THE
BYE BYE MAN

THE
BYE BYE
MAN

And Other Strange-but-True Tales

ROBERT DAMON SCHNECK

PREVIOUSLY PUBLISHED AS
*The President's Vampire:
Strange-but-True-Tales
of the United States*

A TarcherPerigee Book

tarcherperigee

An imprint of Penguin Random House LLC
375 Hudson Street
New York, New York 10014

Originally published by Anomalist Books as *The President's Vampire* in 2005
First published by TarcherPerigee as *The Bye Bye Man* in 2016

An earlier version of the chapter entitled "The President's Vampire" appeared in *Fortean Times*, November 2004. "The God Machine" was first published in *Fortean Times*, June 2002, and a portion of "The Bye Bye Man" (previously published as "The Bridge to Body Island") appeared in *Swank*, February 2002.

"After 18 Years, Missing Teens' Bodies Found in Submerged Van," March 3, 1997, is reprinted with permission of The Associated Press.

Tarcher and Perigee are registered trademarks, and the colophon is a trademark of Penguin Random House LLC.

Most TarcherPerigee books are available at special quantity discounts for bulk purchase for sales promotions, premiums, fund-raising, and educational needs. Special books or book excerpts also can be created to fit specific needs. For details, write: SpecialMarkets @penguinrandomhouse.com.

Library of Congress Cataloging-in-Publication Data
Names: Schneck, Robert Damon, author.
Title: The Bye Bye Man : and other strange-but-true tales of the United States of America / Robert Damon Schneck.
Other titles: President's vampire.
Description: New York : TarcherPerigee, 2016. | Originally published: San Antonio, Tex. : Anomalist Books, c2005. | Includes bibliographical references and index.
Identifiers: LCCN 2016014347 (print) | LCCN 2016016803 (ebook) | ISBN 9780143129721 (paperback) | ISBN 9781101993361
Subjects: LCSH: Parapsychology—United States. | Supernatural. | Occultism—United States. | Spiritualism—United States. | BISAC: BODY, MIND & SPIRIT / Unexplained Phenomena. | BODY, MIND & SPIRIT / Mythical Civilizations. | BODY, MIND & SPIRIT / Supernatural.
Classification: LCC BF1028.5.U6 S36 2016 (print) | LCC BF1028.5.U6 (ebook) | DDC 001.940973—dc23
LC record available at https://lccn.loc.gov/2016014347

Printed in the United States of America
1 3 5 7 9 10 8 6 4 2

This book is dedicated with much love,
to my parents,
Beverly and Arnold.

CONTENTS

THE
BYE BYE MAN

INTRODUCTION

"Unbelievable but true events that are beyond scientific understanding, beyond rational explanation. They will whet your imagination's appetite in the startling breathtaking pages of *Impossible— Yet It Happened!*"[1]

The bottom shelf of my bookcase is devoted to a single genre (or sub-genre) of literature known as the "strange-but-true." I have about a dozen of them there including Frank Edwards' seminal *Stranger Than Science*, along with his rivals and imitators—*Strange Monsters and Madmen; Impossible—Yet It Happened!; "Things"; More "Things"; Ghosts Ghouls & Other Horrors; Vampires, Werewolves and Ghouls; This Baffling World; No Earthly Explanation; Strange Encounters with Ghosts; Strange Guests; Strange Disappearances; Strange Unsolved Mysteries*; and *Strangely Enough!* It's not a pretty collection, and it wouldn't look good under glass, but their shabbiness is a testament to being read. If I understood *The Velveteen Rabbit* correctly, it's the most loved toys that are left in the worst shape and the same applies to books. Every dog-eared page, cracked spine, and water-damaged cover is visible evidence of being carried around in book-bags with half-eaten peanut-butter sandwiches and read at the dinner table, in the bathtub, and discreetly during math class (I missed fractions completely). As for quality, they're mostly hackwork, with the contents lifted from back issues of *Fate* magazine and laid out in the pattern set by Frank Edwards: take dozens of bizarre and/or inexplicable stories, retell them in two or three pages, and top it off with a lurid title.

Some are paranormal ("The Hep Poltergeist That Dug Rock

and Roll," "Tennessee's Horrible Wart Monster," "Cigar in the Sky") but there are also unexplained disappearances, natural and historical mysteries, gruesome murders, peculiar ideas (like perpetual motion, the hollow Earth), and even unusual diseases ("The Boy Who Died of Old Age"). I loved them all, and they became part of the permanent furniture of my mind.

Not everyone shared my enthusiasm. Teachers, for example, were more interested in the principle exports of Bolivia than the nine basic categories of sea serpents, an attitude that baffled me then and still does today. Also, young readers would be well advised to avoid these subjects in their schoolwork; too many papers on vampire-killing techniques, headless ghosts, or living dinosaurs in the Congo, and you'll be taken to an office where people with soothing voices show you inkblots. Many still consider a fascination with strange subjects to be a symptom of maladjustment, and even I am considered a bit eccentric, a perception reinforced by nocturnal lemur-like habits, numerous obsessions, and several phobias.

I Digress

Strange-but-true stories have been recorded since people began writing. Ancient literature is full of wonders, and chroniclers of the period did not see the fantastic as somehow separate from subjects like politics and war. For example, Herodotus, "The Father of History," described races of monstrous men, swarms of winged snakes, "gold-guarding Griffins," and countless other marvels. Medieval and renaissance tales are top-heavy with miracles, and the Revs. Increase and Cotton Mather continued the collecting of "Memorable Providences" in the New World. The nineteenth century turned out numberless pseudoscientific and spiritualist books, along with pamphlets describing local oddities and the "true histories" sold by sideshow performers, most of whom were apparently captured after a bloody struggle in the jungles of Borneo. Cartoonist Robert L. Ripley's popular newspaper column, "Believe It or Not!" first appeared in 1918, but for many the modern era of strange-but-true writing began a year later with the publication of Charles Hoy Fort's *The Book of the Damned*.

Fort (1874–1932) was a journalist and novelist from Albany, New York, who spent most of his time in libraries copying down the anomalies reported in newspapers, magazines, and scientific journals. He was not too discriminating about sources, but the sheer quantity of data are startling, and *The Book of the Damned* was followed by three more; *New Lands* (1923), *Lo!* (1931), and *Wild Talents* (1932). Fort was interested in producing something more than entertaining collections, however, and the "damned" he referred to were those things that had been excluded or ignored by science.

Mysterious phenomena suggest that laws of nature are not fully understood, but Fort took an extreme position, writing, "I conceive of nothing in religion, science or philosophy, that is more than the proper thing to wear, for a while." In other words, everything is somewhat true, somewhat false, and always changing.

Fort was also a wag and offered waggish solutions for the mysteries he collected. How were the pyramids built? "I now have a theory that the Pyramids were built by poltergeist-girls,"[2] meaning by telekinesis. Astronomers see a dark object moving through space; it might be an asteroid but Fort suggests it could also be, "a vast, black, brooding vampire."[3] He even had an elegant explanation for how werehyena-ism might work: ". . . there is no man who is without the hyena-element in his composition, and that there is no hyena that is not at least rudimentarily human . . . it may be reasoned that, by no absolute transformation, but by a shift of emphasis, a man-hyena might turn into a hyena-man."[4] In addition, Fort coined the word "teleportation" and invented a game called super-checkers.

His influence on me was indirect because the books contained sentences like "A barrier to rational thinking, in anything like a final sense, is continuity, because of which only fictitiously can anything be picked out of a nexus of all things phenomenal, to think about." These came along often enough to be discouraging, and I drifted back to the cheap strange-but-true literature that historian T. Peter Park has described as "gee-whiz pop forteanism."

"AN AMAZING BOOK OF FANTASTIC YET VERIFIED TRUE EVENTS . . ."[5]

Tracking Down the Strange

In time, the gee-whiz paperbacks gave way to more substantial reading and vanished beneath accumulating layers of books until they formed the trilobite stratum of my library. Works by Rupert T. Gould, Bernard Heuvelmans, and Ivan Sanderson succeeded them and strongly influenced my own approach to writing. I try to authenticate as much of the material as possible and discuss aspects of it in relationship to history, the paranormal, crime, folklore, science, or anything else that contributes to the making of a "large and fruitful disorder." Failing that, I will settle for an interesting sprawl, but unlike Fort, anomalies are my way of discovering unfamiliar corners of reality, not evidence for overturning conventional views of it.

While looking into the history of Pedro the mummy, for instance, I expected to learn that the popular version was distorted, and possibly a hoax. There were elements of this, but research also turned up surprising aspects of folklore, science, and the things people did to survive during the Great Depression, including amateur prospecting, looting ancient sites, and carving pygmy heads out of turnips. With the discovery of a second mummy, however, Wyoming's local oddity seems poised to go even further, jumping from the pages of *Stranger than Science* to the science textbooks.

Solid physical evidence is almost unknown in cases of paranormal phenomena—a void that is normally filled by speculation. Should someone read this book in 2105, they will probably regard my faith in the rickety findings of parapsychology with the same mixture of amusement and condescension we feel for the writer of 1905 who explained the paranormal in terms of Spiritualism and who, in turn, felt the same way about the theories based on witchcraft and demons that were current in 1805. History shows that interpretations of the paranormal fall in and out of favor, while the paranormal itself continues to flap along being whatever it is and cocking a snoot at those that would explain or control it.

Since the strange-but-true is essentially a collection of old stories, an historical approach seems more appropriate than a scientific one. For the researcher, this means digging through libraries and archives, collecting accounts, comparing them to documented facts, and whenever possible, tracking down primary sources. Sometimes these can't be found, but the research gods are generous and reward the diligent in other ways. Books open to the right page, strangers write with information, and wonderful stories drop out of the sky like fish and frogs. While piecing together the history of the Phantom of O'Donnell Heights, for example, I found what sounded like an encounter between a Mad Gasser and a world famous opera singer.

Bulgarian-born soprano Ljuba Welitsch was the star of the Vienna State Opera and had little in common with the twitchy housewives of Mattoon, Illinois. However, in Vienna, on the morning of July 22, 1951, the maid knocked on Madame Welitsch's bedroom door and got no response. Entering from the balcony, she discovered the room filled with chemical fumes coming from a rug by the bed. It seemed to be saturated with chloroform.

Welitsch was eventually roused and the police summoned, but before they arrived, the rug was washed and "a rare Australian bird, gift . . . from a director of the New York Metropolitan Opera, was dead in the room where the rug had been hung to dry."[6] Police took the rug away for analysis.

The singer said that an intruder must have sneaked into her room, but it was only accessible from the balcony used by the maid and this was thirty feet above the ground. Welitsch had nothing to add except regret for the loss of her "poor little bird."

Was there a mad anesthetist loose in Austria? Had a crime been attempted? Were the singer and her maid concealing something? I have no idea, but the combination of phantom intruders, sopranos, chloroform, and Mitteleuropan policemen puzzling over the remains of a dead bird suggest that something more interesting than waltzing was going on in Vienna that summer.

This is catnip to me and it's why I love studying the strange. Once you start looking, you never know what you'll find. Or what will find you.

1

THE DEVIL'S MILITIA

Gloucester, Massachusetts, 1692

This story is not about ghosts exactly . . .

In 1692, while the Devil was leading an assault on the fractious inhabitants of Salem Village, French and Indian raiders were menacing the seaport of Gloucester fifteen miles away. This was not wholly unexpected; England was at war with France and that meant attacks on the frontier settlements of New England by the French and their Iroquois and Abenaki allies. As recently as October of 1691, raiders had murdered families along the Merrimack River and in Rowley not far from Salem Village,[1] so when strange men were seen lurking in the woods around Gloucester, the people armed themselves and took refuge in the garrison. This was the sensible thing to do, a reasonable response to a situation that turned out to be unreasonable to say the least.

The invaders were bold and for two weeks there were alarms, ambushes, and pursuits, but these French and Indian raiders seemed exempt from the more serious effects of musket balls and, apparently, gravity. In fact, when the raiders vanished they left nothing behind but a bullet dug out of a hemlock tree and some footprints. A short account of the events was written a year later by Gloucester's minister, John Emerson, and his report was included in the book *Magnalia Christi Americana* (1702) by Cotton Mather.

The Rev. Cotton Mather (1663–1728) was one of North America's earliest collectors of strange-but-true stories. (Library of Congress)

Mather was one of New England's most prominent clergymen and shared, with his equally famous father, Increase, a fascination for the "Invisible World" of ghosts, witches, and devils. Today, Cotton is remembered as a fanatical witch hunter and a central figure in Salem's witch hysteria (neither of which is true) and though the *Magnalia* was an "ecclesiastical history of New-England; from its first planting, in the year 1620, unto the year of Our Lord 1698," it ranged widely and contained much more, including a description of a phantom ship that foundered off New Haven, Connecticut, and "A FAITHFUL ACCOUNT OF MANY WONDERFUL AND SURPRISING THINGS, which happened in the town of Glocester [sic], in the year 1692."

John Greenleaf Whittier wrote a lively but very inaccurate poem about these events called "The Garrison of Cape Ann." Whittier described his source as:

> A wild and wondrous story,
> by the younger
> Mather penned,
> In that quaint *Magnalia Christi*, with all
> Strange and marvellous things,
> Heaped up huge and undigested, like the
> Chaos Ovid sings.[2]

Gloucester was founded on Cape Ann in 1623, three years after the Pilgrims landed at Plymouth. It was the first seaport on the East Coast of the United States and an important center for fishing and shipbuilding. It was also a place where wonderful and surprising things sometimes happened. As might be expected in a town that made its living from the Atlantic, these were mostly of a nautical variety: hoodoo ships, fishermen that tended their nets after they died, and numerous sea serpents. The first recorded sighting of a sea serpent in America was made at Cape Ann in the early seventeenth century (it "lay coiled upon a rock . . .") and a many-humped specimen visited the waters off Gloucester annually in the nineteenth century. This inspired the artist John Ritto Penniman to paint an appropriately monstrous nineteen-by-nine-foot canvas showing "a beautiful representation of the City and Harbour of Cape Ann, or Gloucester, and the various Boats which were engaged in the pursuit of this Monster, which is in full view."[3] The piece was displayed in Philadelphia in 1819, but seems to have disappeared. (Another painting, Elihu Vedder's *The Lair of the Sea Serpent* of 1864, shows an enormous silver snake lying on a beach, a sinister image that recalls the first sighting at Cape Ann.) At one time, the pastor of the town's Universalist Church was the Rev. John Murray Spear, who went on to conduct one of the more eccentric experiments in the history of Spiritualism (see Chapter 3: "The God Machine").

Gloucester also had its share of witches and whatever one chooses to call the raiders. While it's difficult to say what they were, we do know where and when they were. They first appeared in a remote part of east Gloucester near the present-day Rockport border, in the vicinity of modern Witham Street. This was known as the "Farms" in 1692, and was home to the Babson family: Ebenezer, a bachelor in his mid-twenties, his mother, and other assorted relations.

According to Rev. Emerson, strange things began happening around the end of June or beginning of July, when the Babsons began hearing noises at night. It sounded like "persons were going and running about [Ebenezer's] house."[4] Then, on July 7, the situation grew more worrisome.[5]

Ebenezer came home late that night. As he approached the house, two men came out the door and ran into a nearby stand of corn (it's unclear whether this refers to wheat or maize). His family said that no one had been inside, but Ebenezer picked up a gun and set out after the strangers. He hadn't gone far when the men started up from behind a log and disappeared into a little swamp saying, "The man of the house is come now, else we might have taken the house."

The Babsons set out for the garrison, a fortified building nearby, and had presumably secured the door behind them when men were heard stamping around the building. Ebenezer ran outside with his gun and saw two men running down the hill and into a swamp.

This would be the pattern of things for the better part of a month:

defenders chasing invaders, invaders chasing defenders, with lots of shouting and firing of guns, but little in the way of results.

On the night of July 9, Ebenezer was walking towards a meadow when two figures came running towards him. According to Babson, they looked like Frenchmen and since one was carrying a "bright gun" on his back, he retreated to the garrison. Inside, they heard the sounds of stamping and running once again. One or two nights later, there was also a noise like stones "being thrown against the barn"[6] (so, there must have been a barn nearby).

At this point, the entire neighborhood seems to have been sleeping in the garrison. This was probably a fortified house built on a hill, with thick walls made of stone or squared-off lumber. A second story normally projected over the lower floor of a garrison by two to three feet and "This overhang feature was designed to combat Indians who customarily attacked with fire or smoke. A loose board in the overhang could be removed in order to pour boiling water on marauders or on fires below. Each wall also had narrow slits for firearms."[7] It also seems to have been protected by some kind of fence or a palisade built of upright logs. When settlements were in danger, citizens worked with weapons close at hand during the day, and returned to these small fortresses at night.

There is no mention of anyone else seeing the raiders until Babson and a man named John Brown were in the garrison and three of the interlopers appeared. They fired on them but "were disappointed by their running to and fro from the corn into the bushes." This went on for the next two or three nights but, in all that time, neither Babson nor Brown were able to hit one.

The Gloucesterites were about to have a violent confrontation with the raiders. When it was over, though, they may have wondered what they were fighting.

The men were in the garrison on July 14, when a half-dozen invaders were sighted within "gun-shot." One stayed behind, probably to protect the families inside, while the rest took off after them. Mather (or Emerson) says the settlers "marched" towards them, but that suggests discipline in what was, most likely, a chaotic scene.

Two of the strangers ran out of the bushes and Babson tried shooting them, but his gun did not fire. They returned to the bushes and he called to the men on the other side of the swamp, saying, "Here they are! Here they are!" Running to meet the other defenders, Babson saw "three men walk softly out of the swamp by each other's side: the middlemost having on a white waistcoat." He got within thirty to fifty feet of the trio, fired, and they all fell down. Shouting that "he had kill'd three! He had kill'd three!" Babson ran towards the spot where they had fallen. Then things got complicated.

He had almost reached the place when "they all rose up, and one of them shot at him, and hearing the bullet whist by him, he ran behind a tree, and loaded his gun, and seeing them lye behind a log, he crept toward them again, telling his companions, 'they were here!' So his companions came up to him, and they all ran directly to the log with all speed; but before they got thither, they saw them start up, and run every man his way; one of them run into the corn, whom they pursued and hemm'd in: and Bapson [sic] seeing him coming toward himself, shot at him as he was getting over the fence, and saw him fall off the fence on the ground, but when he came to the spot he could not find him. So they all searched the corn; and as they were searching, they heard a great discoursing in the swamp, but could not understand what they said; for they spoke in an *unknown tongue*."

Returning to the garrison, the men could see the invaders "skulking among the corn and bushes, but could not get a shot at them."

The next day's devilments began at sunrise, when one of the raiders came out of the swamp and stood close to "the fence" (the fence around the garrison?) within range of the occupants. Isaac Prince took a long gun and fired swan shot at the stranger, but it had no effect and the figure ran off.[8]

This must have been frustrating. In Whittier's poem, one of the defenders loses patience with standard ammunitions and makes an experiment.

"Ghosts or witches," said the captain,
"thus I foil the Evil One!"
And he rammed a silver button, from his
doublet down his gun.

The poet's captain, however, has no more luck with a silver button than a lead ball. There is no mention of the settlers using this method against the raiders, though their descendants used buttons to bring down an occasional witch. In 1745, for example, someone in Gloucester shot a crow in the leg with a silver sleeve button and, at the same time, a local witch named Peg Wesson fell and broke her leg.[9] The doctor was called and discovered the button in Peg's wound. In 1692, however, they needed something more practical, like reinforcements.

Babson, with his knack for running into the invaders, may not have been the best person to send for help. It was two and a half miles to Gloucester Harbor and he had only gone one-fifth that distance when he heard a gun go off. The bullet "whist" past his ear, cut off a pine bush, and lodged in a hemlock tree. Looking around, Babson saw four armed men hurrying towards him, so he ran into the bushes, shot at them, and kept running until he reached the harbor. Six men, more or less, returned with Babson and combed the woods as they went. They saw the pine bush clipped by the bullet along with the spot "where it lodg'd in the hemlock-tree, and they took the bullet out, which is still to be seen." The raiders' footprints were discovered around the garrison, and while the men examined these, they saw an Indian wearing "a blue coat, and his hair ty'd up behind," standing by a tree and watching them. The group "spake to each other" (perhaps calling each other's attention to the stranger), and he disappeared into the swamp. They chased after, fired a shot without results, and briefly spied another figure resembling a Frenchman.[10]

A similar episode took place that day or Mather gives another version of the same story. ("July 15. Ezekiel Day being in a company with several others, who were ordered to scout the woods, when they came to a certain fresh meadow, he saw a man which he apprehended to be an Indian, cloathed in blue; and as soon as he saw him start up and run away, he shot at him; whereupon he saw another rise up a little way off, who also run with speed; which together with his companions, diligently sought after them, they could not find them.")

In a separate incident, John Hammond was scouting the woods with several men when a figure was seen wearing "a blue shirt and white breeches, and something abut his head; but could not overtake him."[11]

Three or four raiders approached the garrison on July 17, but the defenders could not get a shot at them. Richard Dolliver and Benjamin Ellary left the safety of the building to spy on the intruders and what they saw was very odd. Dolliver and Ellary claimed that "several men come out of an orchard, walking backward and forward, and striking with a stick upon John Row's deserted house, (the noise of which was heard by others at a considerable distance;) Ellary counting them to be eleven in all . . ." Dolliver shot into the group "where they stood thickest" but none fell and the raiders fled the scene and were soon out of sight.[12]

The news of invasion that Ebenezer Babson carried to Gloucester Harbor eventually reached Ipswich and on July 18 help was on the way. A Major Appleton sent sixty men "for the town's assistance under these *inexplicable alarms* which they had suffered night and day, for about a fortnight together . . ." Among these men was John Day, who traveled with the company from Ipswich and Gloucester to relieve the garrison. When they arrived, shots were heard coming from the nearby swamp, so they ran in the direction of the sound and Day saw a man with bushy black hair wearing a blue shirt, who came running out of the swamp and into the woods. Day chased him and got close enough to shoot, but the forest was thick and he was unable to fire. The bushy-haired man escaped and when Day "went to look for his track, he could find none, though it were a low miry place that he ran over."[13]

The cavalry, so to speak, had arrived but the invaders did not retreat just yet and Ebenezer Babson was given one last shot at his peculiar antagonists. Sometime around July 25, Babson was in the woods getting his cattle when he saw three of the men standing on a point of rocks that looked out on the sea.[14] One of them had a gun on his back, so Ebenezer decided to ambush the party. He crept through the bushes until he was within forty yards of his targets, took aim, pulled the trigger and . . . nothing happened. Babson pulled the trigger a dozen times, but it did not fire and the three came walking towards him in a leisurely way. They did not menace Babson, they did not, in fact, "take any more notice of him, than just to give him a *look*; though he snapt his gun at them all the while they walked toward him, and by him: neither did they quicken their pace at all, but went into a parcel of bushes and he saw them no more." After this maddeningly nonchalant exit, Babson went home, where "he snapt his gun several times, sometimes with but a few corns of powder, and yet it did not once miss fire. After this, there occurred several strange things; but now, concluding they were but spectres, they took little further notice of them."[15]

Rev. Emerson had more examples of the invaders' mischief, but Mather, an experienced sermonizer, may have decided that the point was made and concluded the account, saying that the statements had been "sworn before one of their majesties' council."[16]

The phantom marauders neatly combined two anxieties that were preying on the minds of colonial New Englanders in 1692. First, there was a fear of the supernatural that is difficult for us to fully understand, but which frightened people so badly that they hanged their neighbors on the word of hysterical girls. Then there was the threat of foreign invasion, which meant homes and farms burned, people taken hostage, and settlers tortured and killed. This suggests the entire episode was mass hysteria brought on by these fears, which sounds like a solution but explains very little.

What if the raiders were real? In that case, a group of armed men spent two weeks panicking eastern Gloucester for no obvious reason and at some risk to themselves. There was apparently nothing strange in the visitors' appearance; the men with black hair and blue clothing may have resembled Indians the settlers knew, and hearing them speak in an "unknown tongue" would not have caused surprise. The others may have been identified as French because they looked like Europeans, wore waistcoats, and were the logical nationality for European-looking invaders in New England. However, none of the witnesses claim to have heard them speaking in French. The only intelligible statement was in English, "The man of the house is come now," etc.

Assuming it was a genuine raiding party then:

- Why were no buildings burned, residents harmed, or property stolen? The invaders were not blamed for the disappearance of a single chicken. The same question applies if the intruders were a gang of English-speaking outlaws.
- Why weren't the raiders seen anywhere else? All of New England was alert to the danger of invasion.
- No campfires were seen or campsites found. Could eleven men spend two weeks in the vicinity without leaving any more evidence of their presence than some tracks, a broken branch, and the bullet found on July 15? The citizens of Gloucester were not indifferent to the question of physical evidence and preserved the bullet, "which is still to be seen."[17]

Unreliable memories and gaps in the records may answer some of these questions, but what the invaders are supposed to have done is just as baffling as what they didn't do. Their most purposeful actions were shooting at Ebenezer Babson twice and missing both times. Otherwise, they spent their time banging and stamping around, drawing the colonists' fire, and being chased after. When the invaders were spied upon, they were seen walking back and forth, hitting John Row's house with a stick. Then there was the inexplicably blasé departure of the three figures under Ebenezer Babson's gun.

Gloucester's official town records "shed no light on this thorny thicket"[18] of questions but a hoax is unlikely. The townsmen would have needed some very compelling reason to deceive or suborn their elderly minister Rev. Emerson and then perjure themselves before royal officials. This was not their idea of a good joke.

New Englanders took the Dark Man seriously and if anyone

needed reminding, Bridget Bishop was hanged as a witch the previous month at Salem Village. Another possibility is that the citizens feared invasion and invented the story so an armed militia might be stationed in Gloucester, but this is also improbable. The Indian War of 1675 had shown that it was not vulnerable to raids. "The isolated situation of the town, bounded on the west by a tract of country too thickly peopled to be crossed by the enemy, and, on every other side, protected by the sea, must have saved it from great apprehensions of assault, though not, perhaps, from some degree of alarm. In all this troubled period there is no record that any hostile Indian set foot on our soil . . ."[19] (The garrison was probably built during this unsettled period.) And, if the Gloucesterites wanted protection, why make the invaders specters?

Some find Ebenezer Babson's apparent "monopoly of these occurrences" to be suspicious.[20] They suggest that his visions of "ethereal French and Indians haunting his community at night"[21] started a panic, but it's hard to see how panic could so distort the senses of Richard Dolliver and Benjamin Ellary that they were able to count eleven raiders. As for Babson himself, there's little information to help us form an opinion beyond saying that he was one of those people that things happen to.

Born to James and Eleanor Babson in Gloucester on February 8, 1667, he never married, paid his taxes, and died young (sometime before 1696[22]). On the night they ran for the garrison, Ebenezer was living with his widowed mother, "an unmarried sister and possibly a married sister with her husband and infant son."[23] As for his temperament, he spent most of the siege running, yelling, and shooting (or trying to shoot) the specters, which suggests he was not the phlegmatic type. Babson's solitary encounters with the raiders are unverifiable, but consistent with other witnesses' descriptions and he never claimed to do anything heroic. No opinions survive concerning his marksmanship.

The Sandy Bay Historical Society has a drawing of Ebenezer Babson that shows him as a kind of Puritan Barney Fife with a steeple-crowned hat, a Bible on his hip, and an expression of frozen terror.

Ebenezer Babson.

Portrait of Ebenezer Babson, 1896. (Sandy Bay Historical Society and Museum)

The unknown artist made him too old—he never saw thirty—and while Babson may have been excitable and impulsive, he was not timid. A narrow jut of land in Rockport Harbor is named Bearskin Neck in memory of the time Babson "encountered a bear and after a struggle succeeded in killing it with a knife; he then skinned the beast and spread the pelt upon the rocks to dry. From this the spot got its name and it gave rise to a jingle . . . 'Babson, Babson killed the Bear, With his knife I do declare.'"[24]

By September 1692, the phantoms had been gone two months when the Babsons found themselves under devilish attack for a second time. Ebenezer's mother had apparently moved to Gloucester Harbor, where witches began tormenting her and a neighbor named Mary Sargent. It's believed that Babson brought some of the hexed girls from Salem to Gloucester, hoping that their ability to see invisible witches would reveal who was responsible. Two women were accused, Elizabeth Dicer and Margaret Prince, mother of the same Isaac Prince who fired a load of swan shot at the raiders.[25] They were arrested, taken to Salem, accused of more witchery, and jailed at Ipswich, where they spent many awful months before being released.

Gloucester escaped the worst of the witch mania and the episode of the raiders has received little attention. Unlike Salem, where explanations have been proposed ranging from sexual repression to ergotism, almost no effort has been made to explain what happened at Cape Ann. Pastor Emerson hoped that "what is written will be enough to satisfie all rational persons that Glocester was not alarumed last summer for above a fortnight together by real French and Indians, but that the devil and his agents were the cause of all the molestations which at this time befel the town."[26] Cotton Mather was more circumspect, writing "I entirely refer it unto thy judgement (without the least offer of my own)."[27]

If early eighteenth-century clergymen tended to regard strange phenomena as satanic, what can we say about them outside of a religious context? Do the missing footprints, apparent invulnerability to weapons, misfiring musket, and other odd elements fit in with phenomena like ghosts, psi, monsters, and UFOs?

The figures' insubstantiality suggests that they were apparitions, but there is nothing comparable to them in ghost-lore. They looked and acted like raiders, but were unlike most of the military specters seen haunting fortresses, barracks, and old battlefields. Martial spirits tend to be stereotypical ghosts that appear in the costume of an earlier period, show little interest in onlookers, and go about their business without leaving evidence of having been there. Gloucester's raiders looked like men of the time, interacted with a number of different people over an extended period, and left physical, if ambiguous, traces of their presence.

No phenomenon in United States history can compare to Gloucester in the number of people involved, the duration of events, or the apparent normality of the beings described. There have been other paranormal sieges but on a smaller scale.

Bluegrass Goblins

Billy Ray Taylor of Pennsylvania was staying with the Sutton family in the small community of Kelly, Kentucky, in August 1955. Around sunset on the evening of the twenty-first, Taylor went into the backyard for a glass of water when he saw a silvery flying saucer come down near the house. Small goblin-like figures appeared soon after. These creatures measured about three and a half feet tall and had hairless, silvery skin that gave off a greenish glow. They stood upright on two legs and had thin bodies with oversized domed heads, big wrinkled ears that came to points, almond-shaped luminous eyes, a slit mouth, and no nose. Their long skinny arms ended in hands that looked something like large bird-claws.

Unlike the Gloucester raiders, the Kelly goblins/aliens seemed more curious than aggressive. One approached the door with his hands up and was shot at. Others peered into windows and one reached down from the roof to grab Taylor's hair as he stood on the front step. The Suttons had a twelve-gauge shotgun and a .22, and their weapons did not malfunction like Babson's musket (or as electronics are sometimes reported to do during UFO encounters). They spent the next several hours blasting away at the invaders.

"Whenever it [the goblin] was hit, it would float or fall over and scurry for cover . . . The shots when striking the object [goblin] would sound as though they were hitting a bucket. The objects [goblins] made no sound . . . while jumping or walking or falling. The undergrowth would rustle as the objects [goblins] went through it . . . There was no sound of walking. The objects [goblins] were seemingly weightless as they would float down from trees more than fall from them."[28] Elmer Sutton later told his daughter Geraldine that "they really didn't walk, just skimmed on top of the ground, but moved their legs."[29]

The Suttons and Taylor eventually had enough; they got into two cars and drove the seven miles to Hopkinsville, bringing back state, local, and military police from Fort Campbell who investigated the scene. Screens were shot out, empty shell-casings littered the floor, and what was described as a luminous patch was seen in the grass. This quickly disappeared. The police left sometime after 2 AM and the goblins (who would not take a hint) came back to look through the windows until shortly before sunrise, when they vanished for good.

Thirty-one years earlier and a continent away, less ethereal creatures attacked a group of miners in the woods of the Pacific Northwest. In this case, however, the creatures seemed intent on homicide.

Gorilla Warfare

Fred Beck spent years prospecting for gold in the Mount St. Helens, Lewis River area of southwest Washington. He worked with other men, who have been identified as Marion Smith, Gabe Lefever, and John Peterson. They occasionally saw large unexplained tracks and, in 1924, heard whistling and thumping noises in the evenings. One day in mid-July, Beck and Smith were going for water when they saw a dark hairy figure standing around seven feet tall. They fired on it and Marion Smith was certain he had put five shots into "that fool's head" but it ran down a ridge and escaped.[30]

Around midnight, the creatures counter-attacked. The men

were asleep in their cabin when it was hit by a "tremendous thud" that woke them and knocked the chinking out of the pine log wall. They grabbed their rifles, looked through the spaces in the wall, and saw two or three "mountain devils" outside, though they could hear more of them walking around. Large stones were thrown at the cabin and some of them came down the chimney; this went on all night. The creatures climbed onto the roof and it "sounded like a bunch of horses were running around there."[31] They tried breaking down the door, pushing the building over, and at one point a hairy hand reached through a space in the chinking hole and grabbed an axe. Smith turned the blade so it could not be pulled through the gap and shot at the thing. The men held their fire except when the sasquatches attacked, trying to communicate the idea that they were only defending themselves, but the assault continued until shortly before dawn.

The sun was well up before the defenders left the safety of the cabin. A creature was standing nearby and Beck shot it three times with a rifle, sending it tumbling down a canyon. They reached the road, got into their Ford, and escaped, abandoning the cabin along with several hundred dollars' worth of mining equipment. The site was named Ape Canyon in recognition of the event and, in 1967, Beck published an account titled *I Fought the Apemen of Mt. St. Helens*. (The cabin burned down long ago, but the canyon survived the eruption of Mount St. Helens in 1980 and is now part of the Mount St. Helens National Volcanic Monument. An enormous lava tube called Ape Cave is nearby.)

Beck's booklet gives the history of the siege, but he is more interested in the metaphysical aspects of the case. He described himself as clairvoyant and a psychic healer and believed the men he worked with were similarly gifted. They used these abilities to find gold ("The method we found our mine was psychic") and believed they were in contact with spirit beings. Despite the sasquatches' seemingly physical nature, along with the stone throwing, footprints, and axe grabbing, Beck felt "they cannot be natural beings with natural bodies." His metaphysical approach is not easy to understand, but he seems to have believed they were primitive spirits that materialized in the physical world without being real living things. Consequently, they cannot be killed or captured, but it does not follow that they're harmless.

"There was enough physical force present to kill more than the number of our party," according to Beck. "If that fate had fallen on us in 1924, they probably would have found five wrangled bodies and a disheveled cabin, and strange large tracks around the area. Of course, there would have been an investigation, but a so called logical explanation would have been given."[32]

Since the apemen are psychical, rather than physical, manifestations, not everyone will encounter them. The miners were especially sensitive to spiritual vibrations and Beck felt that "persons who are psychic have a degree of involvement in a sighting and help trigger the phenomenon."[33] Other writers have proposed similar theories, and, if they're right, perhaps Ebenezer Babson was Gloucester's "psychic trigger."

Three Paranormal Sieges

Gloucester, Kelly, and Ape Canyon are normally considered three different kinds of paranormal phenomena. The raiders' appearance near Salem during the witch mania has made it a footnote to what could have been an unrelated event. Billy Ray Taylor's flying saucer sighting put Kelly/Hopkinsville in the UFO literature as an early and unusual example of a close encounter of the third kind, but what if Taylor hadn't looked into the sky and seen something he couldn't identify? How would it be classified? (Beck might argue that the sighting itself triggered the appearance of the goblins.) Ape Canyon is considered a classic of cryptozoology, the study of unknown or "hidden" animals, but as researcher John Green points out, "There is no other report of sasquatches engaging in any elaborate form of combined activity, let alone a concerted attack on a human habitation."[34]

Each of these events is something of an anomaly even among anomalous events; not unique perhaps, but certainly untypical, and with some common elements. All three took place in the summer, in wooded areas, and each involved armed civilians taking refuge in buildings and defending themselves from an apparent threat by beings that did not seem wholly physical. The witnesses experienced terror, but there is no record of them suffering any injury, either directly or indirectly. In fact, the only physical contact mentioned in any of the episodes took place when one of the Kelly gargoyles touched Billy Ray Taylor's head. Even in Ape Canyon, where the attackers' intentions seemed murderous, they did no more actual harm than either the inquisitive goblins or musket-toting phantoms. Fred Beck makes the point that "Some accounts state I was hit in the head by a rock and knocked unconscious. This is not true."

It does not follow, however, that these incidents weren't traumatic. The miners never returned to the cabin, the Suttons moved a short time later, and Babson's mother apparently left the farm. In each story the beings were hit by gunfire without leaving bloodstains, none of them voiced pain, surprise, or anger, or had their movements impeded by injury. Beck claims that the last creature he shot may have been killed, but it fell into a canyon so there's no way to be sure; the goblins and raiders went down too, but didn't stay down.

The sieges almost seem like theatrical productions. They are real and not real at the same time, with the audience experiencing genuine terror because it doesn't know it's witnessing a strange and pointless play.

It has been over three hundred years since the phantoms appeared in Gloucester. Little remains from that period, and landmarks like the Babson farm and the garrison vanished long ago.

I wondered if the musket ball found in the hemlock tree, the one piece of physical evidence preserved at the time, was still around. None of the museums or historical societies in Cape Ann knows where it is, but that doesn't mean it's gone forever. The bullet may be in a trunk in the attic of some Babson descendant, waiting to be found, wrapped, perhaps, in the pages of its own history like Hawthorne's *Scarlet Letter*.

While looking for the phantom's fugitive musket ball I was not surprised to learn that another relic has survived the centuries. Mary H. Sibbalds, president of The Sandy Bay Historical Society and Museum, wrote to me saying: "I honestly believe that if anyone in the Babson family possessed what they believed to be the famous bullet, they would have given it to the SBHS. We do have the knife with which Ebenezer supposedly killed the bear of Bearskin Neck!"[35]

2

BRIBING THE DEAD

Morristown, New Jersey, 1788

The story of a fake sorcerer who got rich by convincing imitation ghosts to hand over a non-existent fortune.

One night, on the outskirts of Morristown, New Jersey, forty men assembled in a lonely field and began to march. A few years earlier General Washington's Continental Army may have marched through this same field but that night they were mainly farmers who were engaged in raising something a lot more interesting than either rebellion or buckwheat. Candles threw faint trembling shadows onto the surrounding trees and illuminated the sorcerer who presided over the ritual. He stood beneath an awning, directing the procession as it followed occult patterns of circles, squares, and triangles that were laid out on the ground. Most of the men were tired and the whole company was more or less drunk, but neither liquor nor fatigue could make them forget the doom that awaited any who stepped outside the protective boundaries of the diagram. Perhaps they thought a careless foot had gone astray when a column of flame burst from the earth, exploding in their ears and dazzling their eyes.

Men, trees, and diagrams were briefly visible in the flash, along with *something* that stood outside the safety of the magic circle, something that was not of this world.

Silence and darkness followed the eruption and the hush continued until a low groaning was heard coming from the direction of the trees. A tortured howl filled the November night and was quickly joined by a chorus of shrieks that lifted the hairs on the assembly's necks and, no doubt, left many of the quietly terrified men wondering if there weren't easier ways of getting rich.

The line separating sorcerers from confidence men is not always clear. Among the Tungus people of Siberia, for example, shamans use sleight of hand in their healing rituals to make it appear that an illness has been actually, physically extracted from the patient's body in the form of a stone. This is a deliberate deception carried out to convince sick people that they are cured and help bring about their recovery. What happened in Morristown is not an example of that sort of thing. The "sorcerer" in this case was a Yankee schoolmaster named Ransford Rogers and the sole purpose of his deception was to squeeze money out of the participants until they squeaked.

Before taking up necromancy, Rogers was a teacher in the town of Smith's Clove, New York. There he became acquainted with two men who had traveled from New Jersey in search of a person who could help them to find buried treasure. They believed it was hidden in a mountain twenty miles to the west of their homes in Morristown, but that any attempts to remove it were doomed to fail "for want of a person whose knowledge descended into the bowels of the earth, and who could reveal the secret things of darkness."[1]

The Set-Up
Schooley's Mountain, which was then known as Schooler's Mountain, is "a veritable range of highlands" in Morris County.[2] According to various rumors, gossip, and legends, riches began accumulating there during the Revolution when Tories and Tory-sympathizers hid their wealth on the mountain. They were followed by patriots, who buried their money, but died fighting the King's

armies and were unable to dig it up. Pirates were said to have contributed to the hoard, though it's hard to imagine a crew of buccaneers humping their doubloons so far inland. If they did, it might explain the six men said to have been murdered where "X" marked the spot; pirates had a reputation for killing members of the burying detail so their ghosts would haunt the place and drive away prospective thieves. It was these ghoulish overseers that concerned the treasure hunters, for, even if they found their prize, they couldn't carry it away without subduing, placating, or otherwise avoiding these spirits.

Rogers soon convinced the men that he was adept in the mystic arts and had powers equal to the task. The schoolmaster made an excellent impression, for he was "very affable in his manners and had a genius adequate to prepossess people in his favor. He was an illiterate person but was very ambitious to maintain an appearance of possessing profound knowledge."[3] (Presumably, Rogers was literate enough to teach school.) The treasure hunters invited him to settle in Morristown where they would find him a position, and Rogers accepted. It's been suggested that his main interest was a teaching job (with, perhaps, a sideline in swindling) but whatever his motives, he would soon display a masterful hand at the art of flim-flam. In August 1788, Rogers had relocated and was teaching in a schoolhouse three miles west of Morristown. In his trunks, among the hornbooks, birches, tri-cornered hats, and buckled shoes, there may have been a copy of Giambattista della Porta's *Natural Magick* and a supply of chemicals, for Rogers knew something about alchemy as well as conjuring.

Good Enough

The sorcerer was a popular schoolmaster, but soon requested a leave of absence to visit his family in Connecticut. This was granted and when Rogers returned he brought another schoolmaster named Goodenough. Goodenough was hired by the school and would secretly assist Rogers during the magical treasure hunt. The wizard's sponsors were anxious to begin work and he wasn't going to disappoint them, or, more accurately, he was going to disappoint them, but not completely. They would get a good show for their money. Rogers would eventually mount displays so elaborate that more help was needed, but at this point Goodenough was, well, good enough to provide the simple spook effects needed at the first gathering of what would come to be called the Fire Club. (It would also be called the Spirit Batch, the Company, and very likely other names that are out of place in a genteel history like this.)

In September, the first eight members of the club met in a secluded house owned by Mr. Lum, a local farmer. He lived in an area so remote it was nicknamed "Solitude," but even in this isolated spot Rogers had the men seal the doors and windows. What they were about to do required more than ordinary privacy, and when Rogers felt sure that no one could see in (or out), he took the floor. The spirits, he announced with appropriate solemnity, had reached out to him. Post-mortem informants had confirmed the presence of immense treasures in Schooley's Mountain and that obtaining them was possible. The process would be complicated and time consuming because Rogers needed to study the spirits and discover what might induce them to resign their guardianship. He "proposed to serve as a medium between the seekers and the guardians of the treasure,"[4] but would not expect the gentlemen assembled to simply accept what he said on faith; to prove that he was a genuine wizard, he would summon up spirits in the company's presence and converse with them at a future meeting. In the meantime, it was essential for everyone involved in the project to behave with perfect uprightness. Immorality of any kind would offend the spirits and could cause the whole undertaking to collapse.

If Rogers' words weren't impressive enough, their effect was enhanced by mysterious rappings on the walls and ceiling that punctuated his speech, and a disembodied voice that said, "Push forward." Everyone agreed that the first meeting was a great success.

The schoolmaster was serving up an intoxicating mixture of greed, piety, sorcery, and secrecy that quickly attracted new members. They were all male; women and wives weren't invited to join, and forty men were soon attending regular meetings where Rogers

The Elizabethan sorcerer Edward Kelley and an accomplice at work in a churchyard. They are probably using spells and incantations to make the spirit reveal the location of a hidden treasure. (Fortean Picture Library)

described the progress of his negotiations with the spirits, followed by refreshments.

Firewater

Americans of the period weren't afraid to bend an elbow. "In matters of drunkenness there was no difference observable between the classes or colonies and not seldom as much liquor was consumed in the ordination of a New England minister as at a barbecue in the South, while the velvet-coated dandy slipped under the table no more readily than the leather-jerkined plowman."[5] Rogers' séances were no less festive and his followers were encouraged to enjoy a good soak that dulled their critical faculties and "raised their ideas,"[6] or, as female impersonators are fond of saying, "The more you drink, the better we look." A colonist's choice of tipple was largely determined by geography and for New Jerseyans the drink was applejack. This is a brandy distilled from hard cider that the locals called "Jersey Lightning." They drank it straight or as Scotchem, a mixture of applejack and boiling water with a dash of mustard.[7] Then came prayers and demonstrations of occult skill.

"At one of the early meetings Rogers gathered the members of the cult into a field near the meeting house and flung the chemicals into the sky before the eyes of the wondering group. They exploded on the night air in a variety of appearances, downright extraordinary if nothing short of mysterious. The design of the hoaxer to play upon the active imaginations of his audience did not miscarry. These and subterranean explosives, previously planted and timed to discharge during the night to enhance their dismal effect and to engender timidity in the souls of the elect, were pronounced by the awed group to be, without equivocation, of supernatural origin and character."[8]

Magician-scientist Larry White doubts that Rogers' feats could have been performed quite this way. He writes: "There is nothing I can think of that one can simply toss into the air to 'exhibit appearances so extraordinary . . .' IF such stuff were used in 1788 you can be certain stage magicians would be using it today. We ain't! AND, because many chemicals we know and use today were unknown in 1788 it is almost inconceivable to me that . . . Rogers . . . would have access to any chemicals that could accomplish this. I put it down to 'legend.'

"Burying a substance that later exploded MIGHT be possible. If I buried a piece of dynamite (which I do not think had been invented in 1788) with a VERY slow burning fuse it MIGHT explode much later. But 1788 is pushing things a bit, so you would have to consider GUNPOWDER which was known then. Possibly a 'firecracker' kind of shell made with gunpowder and a slow fuse . . . but tricky to do.

"Also consider this possibility . . . a campfire is lit . . . Rogers walks to it and tosses some 'elements' into it which flash and burn. Loose gunpowder? The statement that 'he tossed it in the air' may now, centuries later, ignore the fact that there WAS a fire present."[9]

Giambattista della Porta's book[10] includes a recipe that suggests Mr. White is right. Chapter XI of *The Twelfeth Book of Natural Magick* is headed "Fire-compositions for Festival days" and it includes a method for casting "flame a great way."

"Do thus: Beat Colophonia, Frankincense, or Amber finely. And hold them in the palm of your hand, and put a lighted candle between your fingers. And as you throw the powder into the air, let it pass through the flame of the candle. For the flame will fly up high."

The book also contains instructions for making land mines.

In addition, Mr. Lum and other members of the club saw a spectral figure gliding through the air. Like all the wonders, this was readily accepted by the group, which included a Revolutionary War colonel, an "eminent jurist," two justices of the peace, and two physicians.[11] (Historians have suggested that the floating ghost was one of the conspirators walking on stilts.)

Founding Phantoms

The late eighteenth century is often seen as a clear-minded interval between the witch-manias of the seventeenth century and the rise of Spiritualism in the nineteenth. The standard view is that "Apart from the doings at Salem, colonial America has little to offer in the way of occult history,"[12] and one gets the impression that the taverns were full of rationalist, humanitarian, and scientifically inclined patriots discussing electricity and inalienable rights over tankards of ale. Superstition, however, exerted a powerful influence on the minds of many colonial Americans. The widespread interest in alchemy, astrology, ghosts, spells, magical cures, and dowsing suggests that ordinary citizens may have been less like the Founding Fathers and more like their grandfathers, who threw witches into ponds to see if they'd float.[13]

In 1730, for example, a man and a woman in Mt. Holly were accused of "making their Neighbors' Sheep dance in an uncommon Manner, and with causing Hogs to speak and sing Psalms, &c, to the great Terror and Amazement of the King's good and peaceable Subjects of this Province."[14] The accused were bound and dropped into the water, a test known as "swimming." It worked because water "rejected" the guilty and would not let them sink, while the innocent went down. (The Mt. Holly couple agreed to undergo the ordeal on condition that their accusers also did; the results were inconclusive.)

Witchcraft was, in fact, a hanging offense in East Jersey, where the general assembly declared in May of 1668 that " '. . . If any person be found to be a witch, either male or female, they shall be put to death,' which law was reenacted verbatim in December, 1672 . . ."[15]

This particular law did not apply to Rogers, though. He was pretending to be a sorcerer and "Sorcery is an attempt to control nature, to produce good or evil results, generally by the aid of evil spirits."[16] From a legal perspective sorcerers were not necessarily criminals, but witches were; they made a pact with the Devil and used infernal power to destroy people, property, and the Church. It is highly unlikely that members of the Fire Club would have done that for any amount of treasure and, of course, Ransford Rogers was neither a warlock nor a sorcerer. He was a swindler.

Citizens living in rural areas like Morristown may have been more vulnerable to Rogers' tricks, but that does not mean their urban cousins were somehow immune to supernatural charlatanism. Historian John F. Watson describes an incident that took place in Philadelphia, when ". . . a young man, a stranger of decent appearance from the south . . . gave out that he was sold to the devil!

and that unless the price were raised for his redemption by the pious, he would be borne off at midday by the purchaser in person! . . . at the eventful day he was surrounded, and the house too, by the people, among whom were several clergymen. Prayers and pious services of worship were performed, and as the moment approached for execution, when all were on tiptoe, some expecting the verification, and several discrediting it, a murmur ran through the crowd of 'there he comes! he [sic] comes!' This instantly generated a general panic—all fled, from fear, or from the rush of the crowd. When their fears a little subsided, and a calmer inquisition ensued, sure enough, the young man was actually gone, money and all! I should have stated that the money was collected to pay the price; and it lay upon the table in the event of the demand!"[17]

No one in Philadelphia seems to have wondered what the devil wanted with the money or, if they did, the question wasn't asked. Likewise, no one in Morristown seemed to think it odd when the very moral ghosts guarding the treasures of Schooley's Mountain turned out to have greaseable palms.

In Ghosts We Trust

Rogers showed the assembly what a real wizard could do one stormy night, when he conjured up the first spirit. With thunder booming and rolling overhead and wind whistling in the eaves, the sorcerer conjured up a specter that told them how to proceed. First, it repeated warnings that members must behave with perfect correctness. They must obey Rogers in every particular and meet in November to carry out a ritual that was necessary to achieving their aims. This ritual, however, was not without its dangers and anyone who stepped outside the magic circle during the ceremony would be destroyed. This was a sensible precaution considering that Rogers was planning to set off explosives.

The day arrived and the plotters laid out an occult design where the ritual would be conducted in a field in "Solitude." It seems to have impressed the assembly the way a crop circle might today: ". . . a great variety of paths—circular, elliptical, square, and serpentine—

had been marked off in the buckwheat stubble within the compass of a single night. That evening, when the dupes themselves saw these fanciful paths, they were convinced that a thousand men could not have performed the task done clandestinely by Rogers and his assiduous assistants, and they unhesitatingly ascribed it to demoniac power."[18]

The ceremony began at ten o'clock that evening and continued for five grueling hours. The men gathered at Mr. Lum's farmhouse for prayers and alcohol, then moved into the field where they marched around and around the ritual paths in silence. Then came the explosion, the hideous groaning, and finally the secret that would make them rich.

"The spirits informed them of vast treasures which were in their possession, and which they could not resign unless the company should proceed regularly and without variance; and as fortune had discriminated them to receive the treasure, they must deliver to the spirits every man twelve pounds for the money could not be relinquished by the spirits until that sum should be delivered into their hands . . . Now the whole company confide [sic] in Rogers, and look up to him for protection from the raging spirits. After several ceremonies Rogers dispelled the apparitions, and they all returned from the field, wondering at the miraculous things which had happened; being fully persuaded of the existence of hobgoblins and apparitions."[19]

Rogers clearly had a taste for the dramatic, and his exploits have appealed to dramatists. A theatrical version of the story was performed in the late eighteenth century, but the script has disappeared. Morristown historian Donald Kiddoo wrote a dramatic recital called *The Morristown Ghost*, which was performed in 1989 to celebrate the two hundredth anniversary of the hoax, and an opera, *Ransford Rogers, A Reverberating Opera*, appeared in 1971.

After five hours of marching and kneeling in a magic circle, the men were aching but elated. Now they knew how to get the treasure, and their efforts to raise the money soon turned into a kind of contest.

It's not easy to calculate a modern value for the "mere acknowledgement"[20] the ghosts demanded but it was enough to put solid citizens in debt. The spirits also wanted it in silver or gold, which made things more difficult because the paper money circulating in New Jersey at the time was only accepted in place of precious metal at a 25 percent discount.[21] It was next to worthless out of state where the ghosts were planning to spend it. Demand for gold and silver created a shortage and it took all winter for some men to raise the necessary amount in that form. They borrowed at ruinous interest, mortgaged their farms, and sold cattle for a fraction of its value on expectation of the treasures to come.

Rogers was preparing to pluck his pigeons and did not stand idle. There were more meetings, longer prayers, bumpers of applejack, and spirits that rapped, thumped, "gingled" coins, groaned, and encouraged them all to persevere.

Some of Rogers' followers could not raise the money or get it in bullion, but the ghouls were not inflexible. Men who made a sincere effort were allowed to contribute four or six pounds and paper money if silver and gold could not be had.

By March, most of the acknowledgments had been raised but Rogers had to transfer it to the spirits, so the Fire Club assembled in a swamp and left their offerings by a tree stump the ghost had chosen for that purpose. It was a fairly smooth operation, but "as one of the company was returning he missed his foothold and plunged into the mud. Angered by the incident, he resolved to go back and retrieve his money; but he found the money already gone. The spirit had been too quick for him."[22]

After months of anticipation, the ghosts announced that they would lead the assembly to the treasures of Schooley's Mountain on Friday, May 1. The news was no doubt greeted with a mixture of relief and keen anticipation.

While the men's gullibility may seem incredible today, one writer cautions against the reader feeling complacent or too confident that they would see through Rogers' bamboozling. A local astronomer named David Young published a history of the hoax in 1850 and wrote: "It is too common a thing after a plot is discovered, for those who were not duped themselves, to think their own sagacity would have been adequate to its detection in its infancy. Let him laugh first who is conscious of no imperfection or weakness in himself."[23] Furthermore, belief has little to do with evidence; desire is usually enough to transform wishing into believing.

Black Friday

The time must have passed with glacial speed for men who thought they were about to get rich, but the ghosts counseled patience. Shrouded figures visited the most trusted and respected members in the group, calling them from their beds and repeating the usual admonitions about secrecy and morality, exhorting them to be cheerful and have faith in Rogers. Their forbearance would be rewarded.

At last, the day arrived. James J. Flynn and Charles Huguenin describe what happened in *The Hoax of the Pedagogues*: "On April 30, 1788 [sic 1789], George Washington took the oath of office at Federal Hall, New York City, to become our first president. On the following evening forty deluded souls convened in a large prescribed circle in an open field near Morristown to await the appearance of spirits for instructions about locating alleged caches of treasure in Schooley's Mountain. The ghosts promptly appeared at a distance removed from the circle, but it became obvious immediately that the wraiths were in an angry mood. They upbraided the elect with irregular conduct, faithlessness, and violations of secrecy. They manifested terrifying symptoms of irascibility, twisted themselves into hideous postures, and emitted frightening groans. Rogers himself feigned alarm and exercised all his necromantic skill to placate the choleric ghosts . . . The guardian spirits maintained that because the members of the cult had manifested wicked proclivities and animosities, they were debarred for the time being from access to the treasures. Only by recourse to a variety of incantations was Rogers finally successful in dispelling the ghostly visitants. When the elect soon dispersed, their credulity unaccountably survived, and their confidence in the Yankee schoolmaster remained unshaken."[24]

And that is how the affair stood, with the Fire Club's faith in their future wealth undiminished and Rogers and his accomplices enriched to a sum of between eight hundred and a thousand colonial dollars. If it had ended there, the schoolmaster probably could have delayed the payoff, maybe not indefinitely, but long enough to decamp for the Nutmeg State with a chest of swag. There's something about having an improbable success, though, which seems to demand a second try (and a third and fourth).

Ransford Rogers had become acquainted with two young Yankee schoolmasters who, like him, were new to the area. (New England seems to have produced a lot of footloose teachers at the time. Idle hands being what they are, the two may have impersonated ghosts during the club's séances.) In April 1789, they moved twenty miles away, but kept in touch with Rogers and at some point decided to rekindle the Fire Club. It's said that the younger men threatened to expose Rogers, but the prospect of coin may have been all that was needed for the schoolmaster to don the star-spangled dunce cap again. That, and it had to be more interesting than teaching the alphabet to farm boys.

The two conspirators assembled a group, but Rogers was more experienced and selected likelier prospects from Morristown and surrounding areas. This second venture would be conducted much like the first, with spirits trying to dispose of a treasure, and Rogers and an accomplice acting as mediators between the ghosts and those hoping to benefit from them.

Rogers also seems to have had second thoughts about using pyrotechnics to impress his followers, preferring the simpler, safer method of "direct writing." This is a kind of "spirit writing which is produced *directly* [by the spirits], and not by the hand of a medium or through a mechanical device such as a psychograph or planchette."[25] Direct writing became popular seventy years later, when fraudulent Victorian mediums would replace a blank paper or slate with prepared ones containing messages or drawings from the "spirits." Rogers presumably used stage magic and may have consulted Della Porta for techniques in the chapters on "How letters are made visible in the fire," and "How letters rubbed with dust may be seen."

Let Us Prey

The first meeting was probably held in the familiar surroundings of Mr. Lum's "Solitude" farmhouse. This time, the men stood around a table where a package of paper lay open. Each one removed a sheet and handed it to Rogers, who folded it and returned it to them. Then they left the house, walking single file to an area nearby where a magic circle was drawn on the ground.

"Within this circle they paraded, when, unfolding their papers and extending them with one arm, the [sic] fell with their faces to the earth and continued in prayer, that the spirit might enter within the circle and write their directions one of their prayers. Rogers gave the word amen and prayer ended: each one folded his paper and all marched into the house."[26]

There they inspected the papers and were astonished to discover that one of them contained a message from Beyond. A ghostly hand had written that there must be eleven men in the group and that the spirits wanted their usual fee of twelve pounds in gold or silver. This letter was saved to impress potential converts with a sample of the kind of miracles that happened around Ransford Rogers.

Rogers had not been satisfied with the first club; some members had been caught spying on the spirits as they scooped up gold (leaving them somewhat less awe-inspired) and one night someone had actually stolen the ghost's acknowledgment! Rogers was not taking chances this time. He was determined to defraud no one except "aged, abstemious, honest, simple church members" who could be trusted.

In June 1789, Rogers draped himself in a sheet and made a late night call on one such pious prospect. He roused the startled man from his bed and explained that this was not an ordinary ghostly visitation, but something in the nature of a business proposal. The phantom explained that it was in charge of an immense treasure and was trying to transfer the wealth to a local group, but "could not relinquish it until some church members should unite with them, whose names he mentioned."[27]

The schoolmaster had chosen well. His candidate swallowed the story like an exceptionally wide-mouthed bass and communicated the offer to those church members the ghost had named. They were enthusiastic and Rogers began holding séances again with a new, more religious, tone that appealed to these pious men. So many wanted to join, however, that the club was expanded to twenty-six members with a potential payoff of 312 pounds.

Psalm singing and spirit phenomena were an effective combination, but liquor was part of Rogers' program, and he hit on an ingenious method for striking these sober old men with "Jersey Lightning." The spirits, he explained, had instructed him to make up pills. "Each member was to take one of the pills at every meeting, and to drink freely in order to prevent any disastrous effect, as otherwise it would cause his mouth and lips to swell."[28] Many were overcautious, and if their speech was slurred after a long evening of communing with the spirits, it wasn't from swollen mouths. Some could barely stagger home, where their wives sat worrying about this strange, unprecedented, and inexplicable behavior.

Thirty-seven men were finally enrolled. The plotters donned their sheets once more, keeping the pressure up with nocturnal visits intended to strengthen the company's faith. Meanwhile, the spirits had decided to accept printed currency, so "Rogers told his followers that they must collect paper money and have it burned, in return for which they would receive a hundred fold in precious metals."[29]

When it came time to collect these offerings, the schoolmaster probably stood before the company and received their money. He would have made a great show of wrapping the bills (actually, paper cut to size) in a cloth and then, with a dramatic gesture, flung it into the fire to be consumed before their eyes, a perennial bit of bunco artistry known as the "handkerchief switch."[30]

With most of the money collected, everyone was happy; the members of the club would soon be rich and could stop attending terrifying séances, while the plotters were planning to split up several hundred pounds in gold, silver, and paper money. The only ones not sharing in the general mood were the wives, and it was a combination of their disquiet, along with a handful of dust, that brought about the plotters' downfall.

Rogers had invented a spooky bit of business that involved what he described as the earthly remains of their spirit collaborators. These were pulverized bits of bone that had been portioned out into envelopes and given to each man as a token of his membership in the group, along with a warning that the powder must "be preserved inviolate."[31]

It was probably Elizabeth Carmichael who violated it. At the age of fifty-five, her husband, Alexander, was a model member of the second Fire Club. He was a prominent local citizen, owned a gristmill, and had given the ghosts everything they asked for.[32] Drinking and unexplained absences, however, were not part of his routine, and Mrs. Carmichael may have been looking for clues to explain this worrisome behavior when she discovered the packet of bone dust in his clothing. Fearing witchcraft, Elizabeth took the envelope to the pastor, who refused to even touch it. She returned home, and Alexander, upon either finding the envelope gone or being confronted by his wife, said that she had ruined him. Presumably there was a good deal of arguing, tears, and recriminations that night, but in the end Alexander agreed to explain what was happening, on condition that she kept the secret. Elizabeth promised and she did not denounce Rogers. This was devil's work, though, and what kind of wife stands by while her husband risks damnation itself?

The conspirators learned that their secret was out, but remained calm. Maybe they thought the charade would last long enough to rake in the last few pounds; they certainly gave no sign of appreciating that Nemesis, in the form of Elizabeth Carmichael, was gaining on them. Rogers' behavior became uncharacteristically reckless at this time, suggesting either arrogance or the indifference of someone who suspects that time has run out.

One night, when the schoolmaster was in no condition to be impersonating ghosts, he wrapped himself in bed linen and showed up at the Carmichaels' house. Elizabeth took this opportunity to spy and listened to the conversation that passed between her husband

and a spirit that was evidently pie-eyed and smelled suspiciously like fermented apples. The ghost departed and Mrs. Carmichael, who may have been getting exasperated, asked her still unconvinced husband, "Dost thou deem it proper for ghosts to wear silver shoe buckles?"[33] Given time he might have come up with a good reply to this, but the whole situation was about to change.

The dew was heavy that night, and in the morning Carmichael examined the spot where the phantom had materialized. There were shoe prints in the moist ground that led to a fence where it looked like a horse had been tethered. A trail of hoofprints then led him to Rogers' house, but no one was there. The miller followed the hoofprints for another mile and a half, and when he reached the stable of the horse's owner, found the schoolmaster. It's not known if Ransford Rogers was still wearing the silver-buckled shoes, but he was arrested.

The schoolmaster protested his innocence and members of the Fire Club did not lose faith. They had seen the ghosts, read the phantom letters, heard disembodied voices, and even smelled the spirits' sulphurous odor. And, more to the point, Rogers was their only chance of getting the buried treasure, or even recovering their initial investments. One member of the club put up the fifty-pounds bail, freeing the man, but Rogers immediately fled—and was recaptured. This time Rogers made a complete confession. Nothing is known about the other plotters who seem to have made clean getaways.

With numerous witnesses and dozens of victims, prospects looked bleak for the ersatz necromancer, but he was never put on trial. Rogers slipped away again, possibly with the connivance of men who preferred to keep their involvement with sorcerers and ghosts from becoming public knowledge. As for the club members' "acknowledgments" to the ghosts, "The whole amount of money obtained by Rogers, in these nefarious plots, was about Five Hundred Pounds, or upwards of Thirteen Hundred Dollars; none of which was ever recovered by the unfortunate and humbugged company."[34]

And what about the legends of fabulous wealth hidden on

Schooley's Mountain? At least one treasure really did exist, and while it was not fabulous, it *was* buried. A man named Elihu Bond left a box of coins and silverware on the mountain before going off to fight in the Revolutionary War. When it was over, he came home and dug it up.

As for Ransford Rogers, the schoolmaster learned some valuable lessons from this experience. These did not include "Crime does not pay."

Dr. Dady's Magic Elixirs

Nine years later and one state to the west, in York County, Pennsylvania, Dr. John Dady was convicted of swindling through the now familiar means of pretended spirits, magic circles, and false powders. Several accomplices accompanied him in the dock, but not "Rice Williams," "or rather Rainsford [sic] Rogers, a New Englander."

Dady had come to America as a Hessian soldier. After the war, he set himself up as a minister and then became a popular local physician. Pennsylvanians remember Dady as the chief villain of the piece, but no one familiar with the history of the Morristown ghost could doubt who the real ringleader was, or that he had slipped away again.

Rogers and his partner John Hall had been engaged in "plundering the inhabitants of the southern states by their wiles . . ." when they met Dr. Dady.[35] He may have led them to his neighbor, Clayton Chamberlain, and in July 1797, Rogers and Hall visited Chamberlain at his home. In the course of their conversation, Rogers mentioned that he had been born with a veil over his face, and it had given him the ability to see spirits. This veil, or caul, is a fetal membrane with a reputation for supernatural powers. Rogers could command these spirits, and that very day they had carried him from a place sixty miles away. John Hall confirmed this story and their host was intrigued. Then Rogers asked Chamberlain (in what was probably a casual, "oh, by the way" tone) if he would be interested in seeing a phantom for himself?

He was, and they agreed to conjure one up the following day: ". . . they went into a field in the evening, and Williams [Rogers] drew a circle on the ground, around which he directed Hall and Chamberlain to walk in silence. A terrible screech was soon heard proceeding from a *black* ghost (!!!) in the woods, at a little distance from the parties, in a direction opposite to the place where Williams stood. In a few minutes a *white* ghost appeared, which Williams addressed in a language which those who heard him could not understand— the ghost replied in *the same language!* After his ghostship had gone away, Williams said that the spirit knew of a treasure which it was permitted to discover to *eleven* men—they must be honest, religious and sensible, and neither horse jockeys nor Irishmen."[36]

It's not known what Rogers had against jockeys (maybe they weren't respectable), but his attitude towards the Irish may go back to Morristown: "Rogers often visited an Irishman named Stevenson [and attempted] to win his confidence. Stevenson was reputed to have money close at hand. Rogers would incidentally raise the subject of witches, ghosts, and apparitions. But Stevenson was incredulous, and no progress was being made in the desired direction. One evening, after a long talk on the matter, Rogers said, 'Suppose, Mr. Stevenson, if you saw some night, a white figure gliding along, above the ground, as if it did not touch the ground or walk, but move like a mist or ghost, what would you do?'

"'Bejabers, I would use my shelaleh on him!' was the emphatic reply. It is said that the ghost never dared make an appearance to the disbelieving Mr. Stevenson."[37]

Women, of course, were also excluded.

After the ghost made its offer, a club was set up to perform the required ceremonies. Yellow sand called "the power" was distributed in sealed paper envelopes, and messages from the white ghost began appearing on blank paper. A profitable new element had also been introduced, a chemical called "Dulcimer Elixir," that was necessary for the rituals and only available from Dr. Dady.

The club had between thirty and thirty-nine members and fortunately many of them were wealthy because eleven ounces of elixir cost one hundred twenty-one dollars! Another club was formed forty miles away (Rogers seemed to be setting up a franchise), and in addition to Dulcimer Elixir, they needed both "Asiatic Sand" and the fabulously expensive Deterick's Mineral Elixir. Rogers and his wife made this from cayenne pepper and copperas, an ingredient in ink, and used it to anoint the men's heads during ceremonies.

Dr. Dady, however, was new at this kind of thing and soon overreached himself. When it became clear that the men were willing to pay outrageous prices, he got greedy and began charging so much the club's officers became suspicious. Rogers, sensing danger, fled, and the remaining conspirators were soon under arrest.

The doctor was tried and found guilty at two different trials. He received a sentence of two years in the penitentiary at Philadelphia, plus a fine of ninety dollars from York County, and two more years and an additional one hundred sixty dollars in fines from Adams County. The other conspirators were given lesser sentences. Mrs. Rogers, who seems to have turned state's evidence, was released after the trial and presumably rejoined her husband.

There's no way of knowing how many Fire Clubs Rogers established or the number of men he bilked in the course of his career. New Jersey and Pennsylvania alone produced over a hundred victims and some of them, like Benoni Hathaway, were ruined. Hathaway was a Revolutionary War hero and treasurer of the Morristown club, "an office that proved disastrously expensive after the bubble burst and he was obliged to make good on the receipts for money with which Rogers had absconded."[38] By concentrating on those respectable citizens, who were less likely to either lynch him or allow their private foolishness to become public knowledge, Rogers seems to have enjoyed a good deal of success. St. Nicholas may watch over thieves, but confidence men know that their guardian angel is named Embarrassment.

We can only wonder if Rogers was practicing spirit-related scams before arriving in Morristown, or if his inspiration came from the stories he heard about Schooley's Mountain. The answer is likely to remain unknown, as is the fate of the man himself, who was a schoolmaster, grifter, sorcerer, ghost impersonator, and, quite possibly, writer. As the historians, Flynn and Huguenin wrote: "The suspicion that Rogers himself was the author of an anonymous treatise entitled 'The Morristown Ghost,' that appeared in 1792, is well founded. In it the author, who signs himself 'Philanthropist,' claims a place of honor in the annals of Morris County as a public benefactor for his work in dispelling superstition and ignorance."[39]

3

THE GOD MACHINE

Lynn, Massachusetts, 1853

During the Industrial Revolution
some people developed extraordinary faith in technology.

In October 1853, on a hilltop in Lynn, Massachusetts, a group assembled to create the New Messiah. They had not come to pray to it, sing psalms, or take an otherwise passive approach to the problem; they were actually going to build Him out of metal and wood under the supervision of spirits. When the body was complete, they believed it would be infused with life to revolutionize the world and raise mankind to an exalted level of spiritual development.

The spirits had given their God-building instructions through John Murray Spear, a former minister of the Universalist church and recent convert to spiritualism. Born in Boston in 1804, and baptized by his namesake John Murray (the founder of the American branch of the Universalist church), Spear has been described as a "gentle, kindly, ingenuous" man, who possessed a beautiful simplicity and an idiosyncratic mind.[1]

With his father dead and the family poor, young John may have been apprenticed to a cobbler and worked in a cotton mill but, at the age of twenty-four, he became a Universalist minister. By 1830, he was married and had his own church in Barnstable, Massachusetts. Universalism teaches that all souls will be saved, stresses the solidarity of mankind, and "sees the whole creation in one vast restless movement, sweeping towards the grand finality of universal holiness and universal love."[2] These ideas were to influence the course of his life.

Spear was an outspoken reformist on the subjects of slavery, women's rights, and temperance and expressed views that frequently upset his congregation. By the late 1840s, he had lost the Barnstable church and was subsequently driven from churches in New Bedford and Weymouth. In 1844, after delivering an anti-slavery speech in Portland, Maine, a mob beat him senseless, leaving him an invalid for months. When he recovered, he operated a portion of the "Underground Railroad" in Boston, helping runaway slaves get to Canada, and acquired a name as the "Prisoner's Friend" for his work in improving penitentiaries and abolishing the death penalty.

While Spear crusaded in Boston, a strange series of events unfolded in rural New York State that would change his approach to reform. The Fox family—a father, mother, and two young daughters—had moved into a farmhouse in Hydesville in December 1847, where they began hearing inexplicable sounds. Before long, the Foxes found themselves in the middle of what seemed to be full-blown poltergeist phenomena.

Months of noise, especially knocking sounds, exhausted the family. On the night of March 31, 1848, eleven-year-old Kate invited the "ghost" to rap the same number of times she snapped her fingers. It did, and this display of intelligent control led to more communication. The poltergeist claimed to be the spirit of a murdered peddler, and two basic tenets of spiritualism were established: the soul survives death and the dead can communicate with the living.[3] The day that Kate began communicating with the ghost, Andrew Jackson Davis—a visionary writer and healer known as the "Seer of Poughkeepsie"—had a revelation that "a living demonstration is born" and the movement that was to become known as "Modern Spiritualism" (or simply "Spiritualism") began.

The Fox sisters gave public demonstrations of their mediumship and within five years spiritualism was everywhere. Amateurs experimented with spirit communication in home circles and attended séances and lectures by professional mediums. Hostesses were advised to introduce the "fascinating subject of spiritualism [at dinner parties] when conversation chances to flag over the walnuts and wine."[4] Reformers were especially attracted to the way it challenged social and religious orthodoxies, had neither a hierarchy nor articles of faith, and offered what seemed to be limitless possibilities wherever it was applied.

In 1851, Spear left the Universalist church and became a spiritualist. With the encouragement of his daughter Sophronia, he developed his powers as a trance medium and accepted guidance from the spirits of Emanuel Swedenborg, Oliver Dennett (who had nursed Spear after the mob attack), and Benjamin Franklin, a very popular figure at séances. Spirits led Spear on trips to faraway towns, where he was directed to cure the sick by laying on hands or making inspired prescriptions.

That summer he received twelve messages from the late John Murray and published them as *Messages from the Superior State*. He followed this with a series of public demonstrations in which he entered a trance while spirits spoke through him on a wide variety of topics—including health and politics—and delivered a twelve-part lecture on geology, a subject about which Spear claimed to be almost wholly ignorant. The speeches, however, were not well received, as it seemed to be the medium, rather than spirits, speaking.[5]

Spear trusted these spirit advisors without reservation. Among their "projects" was an experiment in which Spear "subjected himself to the most scathing ridicule from his contemporaries by seeking to promote the influence and control of spirits through the aid of copper and zinc batteries so arranged about the person as to form an armor from which he expected extraordinary results."[6]

Despite his efforts, Spear's reputation remained small, while the

Fox sisters held sittings with leading citizens (including First Lady Mrs. Franklin Pierce), and Andrew Jackson Davis became a famed lecturer and author. Spear's fortunes promised to change, however, after a spirit-inspired journey to Rochester, New York, in 1853, when Spear's special mission was revealed. (Rochester is also where the Foxes made their first public appearance in 1849.)

Spear began producing automatic writing, which proclaimed him to be the earthly representative for the "Band of Electricizers." This was a fraternity of philanthropic spirits directed by Benjamin Franklin and dedicated to elevating the human race through advanced technology. Other groups that made up the "Association of Beneficence" were the "Healthfulizers," "Educationalizers," "Agriculturalizers," "Elementizers," and "Governmentizers," each of which would choose their own spokesmen to receive plans for promoting "Man-culture and integral reform with a view to the ultimate establishment of a divine social state on earth." The Electricizers began speaking through Spear, transmitting "revealments" that ranged from a warning against curling the hair on the back of the head (it's bad for the memory), to plans for electrical ships, thinking machines, and vast circular cities.[7] These would come later, though.

The first and most important task would be the construction of the New Messiah ("Heaven's last, best gift to man"), a universal benefit that would infuse "new life and vitality into all things animate and inanimate." Spear—or the Electricizers—chose High Rock as the place to build it. High Rock is a hill rising 170 feet (52 meters) above Lynn, a town north of Boston. Lynn is now a poor city suffering from high unemployment, but it was once a center for shoe manufacturing and has a Lovecraftean history full of witchcraft, sea serpents, spontaneous human combustion, and rioting Quakers.[8] Spiritualism received an enthusiastic reception in Lynn, and some of its most devoted followers owned a cottage and observation tower on the site Spear needed.

High Rock Cottage belonged to the Hutchinson family, who were both spiritualists and reformers. The cottage was a favorite destination for visitors, especially after 1852, when Andrew Jackson

Davis witnessed a meeting of the Spiritual Congress from the tower, and was introduced to the disembodied representatives of twenty-four nations. Spear had known the Hutchinsons when he was minister in Boston and allowed them to rehearse in his church when they began singing professionally.[9] Spear was given the use of a woodshed, and work on the "Physical Saviour" began in October 1853.

Assisting Spear and the Electricizers was a small group of followers that included Rev. S. C. Hewitt, editor of the Spiritualist newspaper *New Era*; Alonzo E. Newton, editor of the *New England Spiritualist*; and a woman referred to as "the Mary of the New Dispensation." The identity of this "New Mary" has never been clear.[10]

Bringing the Messiah to life was a four-step process that began with Brother Spear entering a "superior state" and transmitting plans from the Electricizers. Building the machine required nine months for construction (gestation), and in that time he received two hundred "revealments" providing detailed instructions on the materials to be used, and how the different parts should be shaped and attached. The group was not given an overall plan, but built it bit by bit, adding new parts "to the invention, in much the same way . . . that one decorates a Christmas tree."[11]

Spear's total lack of scientific and technical knowledge was considered an advantage, as he would be less inclined to alter the Electricizers' blueprints with personal interpretations or logic (what remote viewers today might call "analytical overlay"). The parts were carefully machined from copper and zinc with the total cost reaching two thousand dollars at a time when a prosperous minister earned around sixty dollars a week.[12]

No images of the New Motive Power exist, but a description does appear in Slater Brown's *The Heyday of Spiritualism*, and it must have looked impressive sitting there on a big dining room table. "From the center of the table rose two metallic uprights connected at the top by a revolving steel shaft. The shaft supported a transverse steel arm from whose extremities were suspended two large steel spheres enclosing magnets. Beneath the spheres there appeared . . . a very curiously constructed fixture, a sort of oval platform, formed of a peculiar

Picture of High Rock, taken sometime between 1858 and 1865.
It shows the Hutchinsons' houses and the tower. (The Lynn Museum
and Historical Society)

combination of magnets and metals. Directly above this were suspended
a number of zinc and copper plates, alternately arranged, and said to
correspond with the brain as an electric reservoir. These were supplied
with lofty metallic conductors, or attractors, reaching upward to an
elevated stratum of atmosphere said to draw power directly from the
atmosphere. In combination with these principal parts were adjusted
various metallic bars, plates, wires, magnets, insulating substances,
peculiar chemical compounds, etc. . . . At certain points around the
circumference of these structures, and connected with the center, small
steel balls enclosing magnets were suspended. A metallic connection
with the earth, both positive and negative, corresponding with the two
lower limbs, right and left, of the body, was also provided."

In addition to the "lower limbs," the motor was equipped with an
arrangement for "inhalation and respiration." A large flywheel gave the
motor a professional appearance.[13] This was only a working model,

though; the final version would be much bigger and cost ten times as much.

The metal body was then lightly charged with an electrical machine resulting in a "slight pulsatory and vibratory motion . . . observed in the pendants around the periphery of the table."[14] Following this treatment, the Engine was exposed to carefully selected individuals of both sexes who were brought into its presence one at a time in order to raise the level of its vibrations.

Then Spear encased himself in an elaborate construction of metal plates, strips, and gemstones and was brought into gradual contact with the machine. For one hour he went into a deep trance, which left him exhausted and, according to a clairvoyant who was present, created "a stream of light, a sort of umbilicum" that linked him and the machine.[15]

The God Machine. (K. L. Keppler)

It was at this time that the New Mary began exhibiting symptoms of pregnancy, and the spirits instructed her to appear at High Rock on June 29, 1854, for the final stage of the experiment. On the appointed day, she arrived and lay on the floor in front of the engine for two hours, experiencing labor pains. When they ended, she rose from the floor, touched the machine, and it showed signs of . . . something. Precisely what happened is not clear; Spear claimed that for a few seconds, the machine was animate.

The *New Era* was unrestrained. "THE THING MOVES," claimed the paper's headline, along with an announcement that "The time of deliverance has come at last, and henceforward the career of humanity is upward and onward—a mighty noble and a Godlike career."[16] Spear proclaimed the arrival of "the New Motive Power, the Physical Savior, Heaven's Last Gift to Man, New Creation, Great Spiritual Revelation of the Age, Philosopher's Stone, Art of all Arts, Science of all Sciences, the New Messiah."[17]

The machine's movements remained feeble, but this was not surprising in an "electrical infant" and the New Mary provided maternal attention while it gained strength (unfortunately, there's no mention of what this involved). Despite the headlines, visitors to High Rock were unimpressed. In a letter to the *Spiritual Telegraph*, J. H. Robinson pointed out that the New Messiah could not even turn a coffee-mill[18] and Alonzo Newton admitted there was never more than a slight movement detected in some of the hanging metal balls.

Andrew Jackson Davis wrote a long, carefully worded critique of the whole project. While praising Spear as a man "doing good with all his guileless heart" and a fearless defender of unpopular causes, he suggested that Spear had mistaken his own impulses for spirit directives or had been tricked by irresponsible entities into carrying out the experiment. Davis also felt that the precision and intricacy of the machine's construction was proof that higher intelligences were involved because Spear was "intellectually disqualified for the development of absolute science." He also praised the Messiah's excellent workmanship and construction; it didn't move, but it was beautifully put together.[19]

The Electricizers suggested that a change of air would provide the machine with a more nourishing environment, so the Messiah was dismantled and moved to Randolph, New York, where "it might have the advantage of that lofty electrical position." In Randolph, it was put into a shed but a mob broke in, trampled the machine, and scattered the pieces. No part of it survived.

Spear's High Rock experiment may have been eccentric, but it was also characteristic of the period. New technologies profoundly changed nineteenth-century society, producing industrialization, urbanization, the rise of capital, and a middle class whose values came to dominate society. A conservative reaction to this might have been neo-Ludditism, but Spear was no conservative; he was on a Christ-like mission to transform humanity and believed that technology, the most powerful force of the era, could serve spiritual ends.

He spent the rest of his life working for reform and acting as spokesman for the Spiritual Congress. When the spirits began preaching free love, Spear fathered a child by Caroline Hinckley (1859) and, four years later, divorced his wife to marry the mother. They went on a six-year tour of England, lecturing and holding séances, but were disappointed by the lack of interest in radical politics among British spiritualists.

The couple spent several years in California working for women's rights and socialism before settling in Philadelphia, where they lived contentedly until Spear's death in October 1887. He is buried in Mt. Moriah Cemetery.

Did an angry mob really destroy the New Messiah? This would have been an exciting conclusion to a story that seemed headed for an anticlimax. According to Spear, the Machine was dismantled and transported hundreds of miles to the small town of Randolph. There it was housed in a temporary structure until a mob—in a scene reminiscent of peasants storming Frankenstein's castle—destroyed it. Some sources blame Baptist ministers for inflaming local opinion, and the book, *An Eccentric Guide to the United States*, claims the episode took place in a barn belonging to the Shelton family.

Spear's account was reported in the *Lynn News*, October 27, 1854, but is he reliable? Many questioned his sanity, but no one ever seems to have doubted his integrity or suggested he was a charlatan. The Randolph story, however, is troubling because there is no corroboration and it seems like there should be. Randolph historian Marlynn Olson has searched through contemporary sources and found nothing. In 1854, Cattaraugus County, New York, had two newspapers—one Whig, the other Republican—and neither mentions Spear, a riot, a Mechanical Messiah, or anyone delivering anti-Mechanical Messiah sermons. No known letters or diaries mention the event. "I think," writes Ms. Olson, "the whole thing was a pipe-dream of the Rev. J. M. Spear." Perhaps, like so many other failed experiments, the machine was discreetly sunk into a pond or buried in the woods.

If the New Messiah had not vanished, the passage of 147 years would have improved the reputation of both the object and its creator. As a medium, Spear was a failure, but he built a unique, if unintentional, example of nineteenth-century folk art. And if it had actually moved, it would be as surprising as a Papuan cargo cult making an airplane that could fly. Spear had used the vocabulary of technology, not its language, to build a statue that expressed the human urge for transcendence.

4

THE PRESIDENT'S VAMPIRE

Somewhere in the Indian Ocean, May 1866

No matter how you feel about the current Administration,
no one can accuse the president of being soft on vampirism.

Was a Portuguese sailor the first "real-life" vampire in American history? Did the President of the United States intervene and save the first vampire from being hanged?

Charles Fort gives a vivid account of the story in his 1932 book, *Wild Talents*: "Sometime in the year 1867, a fishing smack sailed from Boston. One of the sailors was a Portuguese, who called himself 'James Brown.' Two of the crew were missing, and were searched for. The captain went into the hold. He held up his lantern, and saw the body of one of these men, in the clutches of 'Brown,' who was sucking blood from it. Near by was the body of the other sailor. It was bloodless. 'Brown' was tried, convicted, and sentenced to be hanged, but President Johnson commuted the sentence to life imprisonment. In October, 1892, the vampire was transferred from the Ohio Penitentiary to the National Asylum, Washington, D.C., and his story was re-told in the newspapers."[1]

The *Brooklyn Daily Eagle* article that Fort based his story on was even more lurid:

"A HUMAN VAMPIRE AND A MURDERER."

"The Terrible Record of a Maniac Convict-Removed to an Asylum."

"COLUMBUS, O., November 4—Deputy United States Marshal Williams of Cincinnati has removed James Brown, a deranged United States prisoner, from the Ohio penitentiary to the national asylum at Washington, D.C. The prisoner fought like a tiger against being removed.

"Twenty-five years ago he was charged with being a vampire and living on human blood. He was a Portuguese sailor and shipped on a fishing smack from Boston up the coast in 1867. During the trip two of the crew were missing and an investigation made. Brown was found one day in the hold of the ship sucking the blood from the body of one of the sailors. The other body was found at the same place and had been served in a similar manner. Brown was returned to Boston and convicted of murder and sentenced to be hanged. President Johnson commuted the sentence to imprisonment for life.

"After serving fifteen years in Massachusetts he was transferred to the Ohio prison. He has committed two murders since his confinement. When being taken from the prison he believed that he was on his way to execution and resisted accordingly."[2]

If James Brown were alive today, he would be described as a serial killer and classified variously as organized, disorganized, mentally ill, sexually sadistic, etc., depending on the circumstances.[3] Serial killing, however, was almost unknown in America before the twentieth century, while the history of vampirism goes back hundreds of years.

New England was the center of belief in vampirism as a preternatural phenomenon with outbreaks recorded from the late 1700s to the late 1800s in Rhode Island, Vermont, parts of Massachusetts, and Connecticut.[4] There are also stories from New Hampshire about a scientist who made himself immortal by distilling the Elixir of Life from baby's blood.[5]

President Andrew Johnson. (Library of Congress)

More mundane examples of blood drinking occurred among snowbound travelers and victims of shipwreck who were forced to survive by cannibalism. Sexual pathologies like blood fetishism were discussed (in Latin) by Dr. Richard von Krafft-Ebing, whose *Psychopathia Sexualis* included contemporary European examples ("Case 48 . . . he first had to make a cut in his arm . . . she would suck the wound and during the act become violently excited sexually"[6]). Was James Brown a violent blood fetishist? Could he have believed that he was a genuine vampire?[7]

Brown's story has been retold in books, magazines, and websites, where it's accompanied by dripping red letters and flapping cartoon bats, but these retellings are often inaccurate and offer little beyond the accounts in the *Eagle* and *Wild Talents*. That means the two main sources for these crimes were published twenty-six and sixty-six years after the events they describe.

Could anything new be learned 137 years later? Contemporary newspapers were not likely to have ignored a sensational double murder, and if official records survived, they would provide verification. Fortunately, even vampires leave a paper trail.

The President Intervenes

The commutation was the first important document to be found:

"To all to whom these Presents shall come, GREETING:

"Whereas, at the October term 1866, of the United States Circuit Court for the District of Massachusetts, one James Brown was convicted of murder and sentenced to be hung.

"And whereas, I am assured by the United States District Attorney, Assistant District Attorney, Marshal and others, that there were certain mitigating circumstances in this case which render him a proper object of executive clemency;

"Now, therefore, be it known, that I, Andrew Johnson, President of the United States of America, in consideration of the premises, divers other good and sufficient reasons me thereunto moving, do hereby commute the said sentence of death imposed upon the said James Brown to imprisonment at hard labor in the Massachusetts' State Prison at Charlestown, Massachusetts, for the term of his natural life."[8]

This proves that James Brown existed, that he was convicted of murder, and that the President of the United States commuted his sentence. No mention is made of what the "divers other good and sufficient reasons" for the commutation might have been, and if they had been included we would know more about both Brown and Johnson, one of America's most forgotten presidents. (Despite the turbulence of his administration, Johnson is even more obscure than Millard Fillmore, whose total obscurity has given him a degree of notoriety.)

The commutation led to prison registers, trial records, newspaper articles—even the ship's log—and as these accumulated, James Brown, the killer-vampire, dissolved like Max Schreck in a sunbeam. What remained was not a pile of dust but a run-of-the-mill murderer, whose story bears little resemblance to published accounts.

The following reconstruction is based on the collected documents.

Murder on the High Seas

May 23, 1866, was a fair day with a breeze from the Southeast; pleasant weather for men aboard the bark *Atlantic* as it cruised for whales in the Indian Ocean.[9] The crew spent the day bundling up the whalebone (baleen) that was used in those pre-plastic days for making umbrella ribs, buggy whips, and corset stays. Whalebone, however, was little more than a by-product of the search for whale oil, which was found in the animal's head and blubber and provided the best illumination and mechanical lubricant available at the time. In order to collect it, fleets of ships that combined the functions of a hunting lodge, processing factory, and warehouse combed the seas.

The *Atlantic* was one of them, "a staunch, well-built craft of two-hundred and ninety tons," with a crew of thirty or more men.[10] Brightly painted whaleboats hung from davits, ready to drop rowers and harpooners into the sea at a shout of "There she blows!" (or "There she breaches!" or "There she white waters!"). An enormous brick stove stood on her deck for boiling whale oil out of blubber. Also on deck were James Brown, a "negro cook" from New Bedford,[11] blacksmith James W. Gardner, and seaman John Soares (or Suarez).[12]

Brown was around twenty-five years old. He stood five-feet, six and a half inches tall, had a rounded chin, black hair, and "frank" eyes. His skin was decorated sailor-style with tattooed eagles, anchors, hearts, and stars and, on his right forearm, a woman wearing a skirt.[13]

He was busy scrubbing a pan when nineteen-year-old James M. Foster came on deck from the forecastle. Foster leaned against a cask by the fore swifter and called Brown a "damned nigger."[14] Presumably there was bad blood between them. On whaling voyages lasting three or four years, there was often nothing for the men to do but carve scrimshaw and get on each other's nerves. Quarrels were common and sometimes led to violence, as court papers show.

"[James Brown] wilfully, feloniously and of his malice aforethought an assault with a certain knife of the length of six inches and the breadth of one inch did then and there make, and him the said James Foster with the aforesaid knife which he the said James Brown then and there had and held did then and there strike, stab and wound and in and upon the said James Foster in the left side of the breast of him the said James Foster with the aforesaid knife, so as aforesaid had and held by him the said James Brown, one mortal wound of the length of one inch and of the depth of four inches did then and there inflict, of which said mortal wound so as aforesaid inflicted with the knife aforesaid, which the said James Brown so as aforesaid had and held, the said James Foster did then and there languish, and so languishing did then and there for the space of five minutes linger and then and there so languishing, on the day and year aforesaid, did then and there die . . ."[15]

Soares thought Brown had hit Foster with his fist. James W. Gardner "was within a few feet of Brown when he cut Foster and helped the latter to the wheel; asking him what was the matter but he could not speak, and lived but five or six minutes."[16] Captain Benjamin Franklin Wing had the cook put into double-irons in the fore-hold, where he later admitted to stabbing Foster with a double-edged sheath knife and throwing it overboard.[17] (See Appendix I: "Entries from logbook of the bark *Atlantic*.")

Brown and the witnesses were transferred to other ships and taken to Boston. He was indicted on September 11, arraigned on

October 19, pleaded "Not Guilty" and tried in U.S. District Court on November 13, 1866, with Judges Lovell and Clifford presiding. District Attorney Hillard and Assistant District Attorney Dabney presented the government's case, and Charles R. Train and N. St. John Green conducted the defense. (In an undated letter to President Cleveland, Brown writes that he paid his lawyer "nine barrels of oil at that time oil was worth two Dollars and seventy five cents a gallons [sic]." See Appendix II: "James Brown's letters.") It was a short trial. The jury deliberated seventy-five minutes before finding Brown guilty. He was sentenced to death and President Johnson signed the commutation on January 3, 1867.

Brown was taken from the Suffolk Jail to the Charlestown State Prison, a dreary granite pile where he spent the next twenty-two years.[18] On April 14, 1889, he was sent to the Ohio State Penitentiary in Columbus, possibly because Charlestown was being renovated. Two years later, on November 3, 1892, Brown was removed to the U.S. Government Insane Asylum in Washington, D.C. He probably spent the rest of his life there.[19]

An interesting question arises: how was this very ordinary crime transformed into a harrowing tale of maritime guignol?

The Transmogrification of James Brown

Newspapers of the Gilded Age had a casual approach to facts that allowed them to publish stories that still fascinate forteans; this was the era that produced perennial favorites like the cattle-rustling airship and the pterodactyl killed by cowboys. Furthermore, November 4, 1892, was a slow news day. "A Human Vampire" appeared on the front page between the obituary of Wheaton A. Welsh, "the well known Local Public School Principal," and a shoot-out in Wyoming, suggesting someone at the *Eagle* might have succumbed to temptation and embellished an otherwise uninteresting news item.

It's possible, though unlikely, that the article is accurate and Brown committed two more murders in prison. If so, they could have inspired the copywriter to retrofit the original account and might explain why Brown was sent to an insane asylum. "A Human Vampire" does not go into details. If the murders were in Massachusetts, however, they should have appeared on Brown's record when he was moved to Ohio (the Ohio Prison Register mentions one conviction for first-degree murder, death sentence commuted). Brown might have committed the murders after arriving in Ohio, but by 1889 he was almost fifty years old and suffering from cataracts in both eyes. So far, no evidence has been found to support the newspaper's claim.

Another possibility is that Brown's story became confused, commingled, or otherwise mixed up with another Brown who was in the news that year.

The Vampire Brown

One of New England's most famous cases of vampirism took place a few months before Brown was moved to the asylum.

It began when the Brown family of Exeter, Rhode Island, was almost wiped out by tuberculosis. George T. Brown lost his wife and two daughters, and by 1892, his son, Edwin, was seriously ill. Desperate for a cure, he had the bodies exhumed and examined for signs of vampirism on March 17 of that year. Mrs. Brown and the older daughter were in reassuringly complete states of decomposition, but the remains of nineteen-year-old Mercy raised suspicions. Blood was found in her heart and the liver had not decayed (she was only dead two months and had been buried in the middle of winter). A fire was lit in the cemetery and the two organs reduced to ashes. Edwin may have then mixed these ashes with water and drunk the concoction as a cure.[21]

Was the story of James Brown, the murderer, combined with that of Mercy Brown, the vampire? There are three points in common: both occurred in 1892,[22] have New England as settings, and feature vampires surnamed Brown. This proves nothing, but it does suggest a direction for further research.

Conclusion

James Brown was probably not a blood-drinker. He definitely did not commit the two shipboard murders attributed to him by

Charles Fort or the *Brooklyn Daily Eagle*, and reports based on these sources are inaccurate. Later murders are possible but no evidence has turned up.

It would be interesting to know why the president commuted Brown's death sentence, but whatever the reason, Andrew Johnson's legacy does not include being the only President of the United States to save a vampire from hanging. And even if it did, most Americans would still think he's Andrew Jackson.

Other questions remain. Why was Brown sent to an insane asylum? How did his story become so distorted? And, finally, if James Brown wasn't America's first "real-life" vampire, who was?

His file from St. Elizabeths Hospital contains little about illness or treatment. There are some official documents relating to Brown's transfer and warnings that the prisoner is dangerous (see Appendix III: "How dangerous was James Brown?"), but most are letters from Brown to his doctor, W. W. Godding. There are also letters addressed to a female relation named Emma F. Cary and an appeal to President Grover Cleveland.

English was not Brown's native language, yet most of his letters are reasonably well written and the penmanship is handsome. Some of them, however, make no sense. The same thoughts are repeated over and over, the handwriting is difficult to read, and sentences drift across the page in waves. These changes may have been the result of Brown's mental state, cataracts, poor physical health, or even boredom.

The letters are in two groups, 1885–1887 and 1892, and the first thing we learn is that the original chronology was wrong. Brown spent two years as an inmate at St. Elizabeths before returning to Massachusetts. When he was moved to Washington in 1892, it was for the second and final time. The 1885–1887 series include Brown's version of the murder, why he felt the trial was unjust, and many complaints to Dr. W. W. Godding about the hospital and the attendants, along with requests for supplies. (1887 was also the year Brown's bark, the *Atlantic,* sank; see below.)

In the letter to President Cleveland, Brown claims that his

Dr. W. W. Godding. (Library of Congress)

problems with Foster were over food. Foster was getting less than he wanted, and Brown told him that he was getting as much as Captain Wing had allowed. Foster insisted on more provisions and:

". . . James Foster said to me, I will also make you obey me I then said to him it will be a very cold day. Thereunder he struck me with a belaying pin on the back of my head. I fell on the deck when I got up he struck me again. I saw the blood running on my shirt I said to him what do you mean He then struck me third times I then stabbed him with my knife."

In addition to claiming that the murder was self-defense, Brown stated that his trial had been unfair because the judges would not delay it until the *Atlantic* had returned from its voyage. As for the witnesses, they: ". . . were my enemies for they were not on deck when this occur. They had been sick all the time while they were on board of the Atlantic they could not work and the viceconsul sent them on with me. Two of them were Portuguese and they could not speak the English language. The Judge said to me he cannot postpone my trial because it is too much expense to the government and the Judge would not permit my lawyer to put any questions to those witnesses."

Brown claimed that everyone in the courtroom saw the trial was unfair and that's why his sentence was commuted to life.

The letters he wrote to Dr. Godding about conditions in the hospital and the behavior of attendants make harrowing reading. An undated note, presumably from January 1887, begins: "Mr. Duley beat S. Jackson with an iron rod that evening I heard Jackson said to him for God sake do not strike me any more with that iron rod."

As for the doctor, William Whitney Godding (1831–1899) was considered a leading authority on mental illness in his time. In 1882 he published a book, *Two Hard Cases: Sketches from a Physician's Portfolio*, which includes a psychological profile of President James Garfield's assassin, Charles Guiteau.

We also learn that Brown enjoyed smoking and kept two pet birds named Rosaliene and Susanna, one of which he accidentally killed.

Apparently, he either didn't know or, at that point, didn't care about the newspaper calling him a vampire. If Brown were well enough to understand the accusation, however, he probably would have objected. In a letter dated December 7, 1885, he complains about an article in the June 25 issue of the "evening star" (possibly the *Washington Evening Star*) that said he had killed Captain Wing.

As for his origins, Brown claimed to be born in January 1839, in Georgetown, Guyana, and that he was a native of the now defunct Republic of Colombia, an independent federation of Colombia, Panama, Venezuela, and Ecuador. He said that "New Grenada"— modern Colombia or Venezuela—was his home country and that suggests Brown spoke Spanish not Portuguese.

In 1904, the Superintendent of the Government Insane Asylum received a letter from the Charlestown Prison in reference to Brown. Massachusetts wished to know if James Brown was still alive and if so, whether his mental condition had improved. If he were dead, however, when and where had he been buried? Written across the top was a terse response:

> "James Brown (Col) U.S. Co [obscured]
> adm. Nov. 4, 92
> died Dec. 15, 95
> Hosp. Cemetery."

There Seems Some Doom Over This Ship

Charles Fort wrote that James Brown's story was retold in other newspapers at the time. This raises an intriguing possibility.

Bram Stoker was collecting material for *Dracula* in 1892, the year that the Brown article appeared in the *Daily Eagle*. Stoker is known to have had at least one clipping from a New York paper that involved vampires. It was an account that appeared in the *New York World*, one of the yellowest of the yellow journals, concerning a mother who drank the blood of her four children.[23] Could the novelist have seen the piece about James Brown, too? Did a story about a ship where sailors disappeared one-by-one at the hands of a vampire appear in a British paper like *The Illustrated Police News*? If so, it may have inspired a section of *Dracula*.

The seventh chapter of the book describes the Count's passage from Transylvania to England aboard the Russian schooner *Demeter*. He passes the time by feeding on the crew until no one is left alive and the vessel sinks in a storm at the port of Whitby. Stoker based this on a real shipwreck that took place in the harbor years earlier.

Furthermore, the *Demeter* and Brown's bark, the *Atlantic*, suffered similar fates. In 1887, the *Atlantic* was wrecked off the coast of San Francisco, ". . . surrounded by the impenetrable fog and darkness, with the spars and rigging tumbling about their heads, the stout timbers crunching and splitting like matchwood, and the ceaseless roar and turmoil of the surf as it swept the wreck from one end to the other, the situation was appallingly dreadful, and many of the crew were doubtless killed outright, while others gave up in despair and became an easy prey to the remorseless waves." Twenty-eight of the thirty-seven men onboard perished and the vessel was totally destroyed in "one of the most melancholy and disastrous wrecks of the year."[24]

At this point, the relationship between James Brown and *Dracula* is based on nothing more than a coincidence of dates; literary historians will have to decide if it has any merit.

5

ONE LITTLE INDIAN

Wyoming, 1932

A strange-but-true classic, continued.

Extraordinary human remains have reportedly been discovered throughout the United States. They include the skeletons of men seven feet tall with horns growing out of their foreheads, that were unearthed in Sayre, Pennsylvania, in the 1880s[1]; 75,000 to 100,000 pygmies found in an ancient cemetery in Coffee County, Tennessee, in 1876[2]; and a collection of enormous skulls exhumed with bones and artifacts during a guano mining operation in Nevada's Lovelock Caves in 1911.[3] There are other stories about equally monstrous cadavers, but the bodies themselves have all been misplaced, stolen, destroyed in fires, or swept away in floods. Only two examples are known to be in museums today, the Cardiff Giant and a Lovelock Skull.

The Cardiff Giant was a deliberate hoax. It appeared to be the body of a ten-foot-tall man, which was "discovered" by well diggers on a farm in Cardiff, New York, in 1889. The stone figure was naked, looked uncomfortable, had no hair, and lay in a position that allowed it to be displayed without giving offense. Various theories were advanced to explain the mystery, including that it was a gigantic petrified Indian, an ancient statue, or one of the human/angel hybrids the Bible calls *nephilim*. But it was actually the oversized brainchild of a man named George Hull.

Hull paid artisans to carve the figure out of gypsum and then treated the surface with sand and acid to simulate the effects of erosion. The statue was then buried on land belonging to one of his relatives and spent a year there, "seasoning" underground. A considerable amount of time, money, and thought went into this project; darning needles were even used to cover the figure with holes resembling pores (presumably, this involved holding a number of needles together, and striking the blunt end with a mallet). Creating the giant cost thousands of dollars, and while Hull intended to make a profit, he also hoped to cause embarrassment. Several sources describe him as an atheist and say he had argued with a certain evangelist over the meaning of Genesis 6:4: "There were giants in the earth in those days; and also after that, when the sons of God came in unto the daughters of men, and they bare children to them, the same became mighty men which were of old, men of renown."[4] Whether this part of the plan succeeded is not known, but Hull exhibited the Cardiff Giant with so much success that P. T. Barnum offered to buy it. When the offer was declined, the Great Showman had his own giant carved and put it on display.

Experts soon exposed the statue as an object of recent manufacture, but not until Hull had made a profitable return on his investment. The Cardiff Giant can now be seen at the Farmers' Museum in Cooperstown, New York, while Barnum's copy resides in Farmington Hills, Michigan, at Marvin's Marvelous Mechanical Museum.

While these are artificial objects, the Lovelock Skull is an authentic skull reputed to be "almost 30 cm (1 foot tall), [that] is preserved with some related bones and artefacts at the Humboldt Museum in Winnemucca, Nevada."[5] I asked a very patient lady at the museum about it and learned that they get many inquiries about the skull. It is not on display, and while the skull looks normal, she did point out that "'giant' is a relative term."

When fantastic relics disappear or are kept in storage, it raises suspicions among the conspiracy-minded and the skeptical. The former see it as the deliberate suppression of paradigm-smashing evidence by a scientific establishment intent on concealing the truth. (Hoaxes can be displayed, but true anomalies are kept in the same Smithsonian sub-basement that contains the Ark of the Covenant, pickled Zeta-Reticulans, and certain parts of John Dillinger.) The unbelievers, meanwhile, cite lack of evidence and unreliable accounts, and conclude that the stories are fraudulent or grossly inaccurate. What, for example, can make 75,000 to 100,000 dead pygmies vanish? And why were Pennsylvania's horned skeletons sent to the American Investigating Museum in Philadelphia, when it doesn't seem to have existed? Was this a cover story or a hoax?

Unlike aliens, ghosts, or bigfoot, however, one of these oddities did leave physical evidence behind, albeit temporarily, in the form of a body: the Pedro Mountain mummy.

The Pedro Mountain mummy—or simply, "Pedro"—appeared to be the dried corpse of an extraordinarily small old man sitting cross-legged "like a Buddha."[6] Like other anomalous remains, he was found accidentally, and vanished under peculiar circumstances, but not before acquiring some history. He had different owners, was seen by many witnesses, and was examined by scientists at bona-fide institutions who photographed and X-rayed the tiny body. In addition, he was the subject of a national radio broadcast. One writer has made the reasonable comment, "to tell the truth I'm a little skeptical of the mummy interpretation. It seems much too convenient that the figure has disappeared completely and is no longer available for further scientific examination."[7] But even with these misgivings, Pedro remains a comparatively substantial proposition; this should be kept in mind when either dismissing other stories as too improbable to be believed, or falling back on conspiracy theories to explain why things disappear.

But where did Pedro come from, and where did he go? And if he was real, a real what?

The Standard Version

The most widely circulated version of the story goes like this: in 1932, two prospectors were looking for gold in the Pedro Mountains of Wyoming, when they set off dynamite and uncovered a cave. Inside they found a tiny mummy, sitting on a ledge. The mummy spent the next several years being displayed in sideshows, until a Casper businessman bought it and brought Pedro to various museums. Scientists agreed that he was real and probably the remains of an infant with a fatal birth defect. When Pedro's owner died in 1951, the mummy disappeared, and it hasn't been seen since. Then in 1979 an anthropologist at the University of Wyoming saw pictures of Pedro's X-rays. He agreed with the earlier scientist's interpretation and speculated that miniature mummies may be responsible for strongly held local beliefs in a race of pygmies. Others saw the mummy as proof that the pygmies were (or are) real.

A researcher named Eugene Bashor listed twenty different sources of information related to the Pedro Mountain mummy. Most of these describe how he was found and what happened to him but there are other sources that suggest the story may be more complicated.

The Prospectors

Their names were Cecil Main and Frank Carr. Little is known about Carr, but Main was a very young man from Alliance, Nebraska, and the two of them were looking for gold in Wyoming's Pedro Mountains when they found the mummy in October 1932. (In November 1936, Main produced a notarized deposition describing how it happened. According to this document the mummy was found in June 1934.) They were prospecting in the low mountains that fringe the southern edge of the Pathfinder Reservoir[8] near the town of Leo, in northern Carbon County.[9] (It's believed they were working near the site of a mining road that leads up into the mountain called "Little Man Road.") Main and Carr were "gophering"—making shallow holes in the rock, inserting dynamite, and setting it off— when an explosion exposed the mouth of a small, natural cave that had been tightly closed with stones.[10] It was around four feet high, three feet wide, and fifteen feet deep. When Main crawled inside, he went as far back as the narrowing walls allowed, and there he found Pedro sitting on a slight ledge.

Carr does not seem to have had an interest in the mummy. It apparently belonged to Cecil Main, who brought it to the office of the state historian in Cheyenne, Mrs. Cyrus Beard, hoping that she might purchase it for the state of Wyoming. While in her possession, Pedro seems to have been examined by a doctor who believed the mummy was a premature child, possibly preserved in chemicals. Mrs. Beard declined Main's offer because funds were not available (this was during the Great Depression) and "there was *a lack of authentic records in support of the location of the cave and of the actual discovery*"[11] [my italics].

Eugene Bashor, working from Main's deposition, writes that by 1936 the mummy was "owned by Homer F. Sherrill and it was located in the Field Museum, Chicago, Ill."[12]

There are variations of these stories. Some accounts claim the cave was actually a hollow chamber enclosed in solid rock, suggesting that Pedro was found like a toad in a stone. There are also rumors that three little mummies were actually discovered, but that two of them deteriorated.[13]

Main's deposition raises important questions. First, why did he claim that it happened twenty-one months after they actually discovered it? The find was reported in the Casper papers in October 1932, so if this was intended to deceive anyone, it was not well done. Did he simply forget? Didn't he save the newspaper clippings? Even if he was illiterate, this would be surprising. (Main could certainly sign his name—it's on the deposition.)

Secondly, why couldn't he give the location of the cave? If the prospectors had found gold, would they have been able to file a claim if they didn't know where it was? If selling the mummy depended on this information, why couldn't Main provide it?

Finally, Bashor could find no record of anyone named Sherrill who was associated with the Field Museum, and that institution has no record of the little mummy in their collections (though, they do have photographs). Again, these rumors are easily checked and they turn out to be false.

Main's account (as rendered by writer Frank Edwards) is the best-known version of the story, but his unreliability in reporting basic facts should be taken into account before accepting it as true.

The Miners

Robert Cardwell told a different version of how Pedro was found. He said it also happened in 1932, when his father, Henry, hired striking coal miners from Hanna, Wyoming, to help bring the hay in. The ranch is near the Pathfinder Reservoir and the miners spent their spare time exploring the local caves. Inside a cave four feet high and fifteen feet deep, they found the mummy sitting "on a small shelf two feet high."[14]

Spelunking is a thin man's pastime and it was a miner named "Skinny" Rimmer who gave the mummy to Henry Cardwell. His wife, Winnie, refused to have it in the house, so Mr. Cardwell brought it to Casper, where he showed it to a doctor and a lawyer and left it with the funeral directors at Gay and Horstman. ("Cardwell, who was the only Republican amongst his friends, stated jokingly, 'He must have been a Democrat, you can tell by the shape of his head.'"[15]) But did he simply abandon it? An article in *Argosy* later reported that "Winnie Cadell [sic] of Alcova, Wyoming . . . loaned a 'little demon mummy' to a college professor. It was never returned."[16]

More Mummies

Other pygmy mummies and the heads of pygmy mummies were allegedly found in the 1930s. A Mexican sheepherder named "Señor Martinez"[17] is said to have found a complete body and six heads near the Pathfinder Reservoir. After losing half his flock in a blizzard, however, he decided they were bad luck and buried the remains. Another version of Pedro's discovery involves a sheepherder.

"Some years ago, either in *The True West Magazine* or the *Frontier Times*, a man wrote an article on the San Pedro Mummy. He said a sheepherder trapper had found it in a very dry cave when he was trapping the wolves and coyotes that were killing the sheep. He took it to town when he got time off and showed it around and sold it for booze to a dentist (I think) for money to buy drink for a big drunk."[18]

A Casper attorney was said to have found a mummy near the Pathfinder Reservoir during a fishing trip, and a local orthopedist named Richard Phelps owned a pygmy head. The most improbable story is a "friend-of-a-friend" tale involving a man who found a cave near the reservoir containing two hundred to three hundred pygmy mummies. He brought one home but his wife made him put it back, and he spent eight hours burying the cave (entrance?). Since then, the cave is supposed to have been flooded several times.

It was also in the 1930s that several pygmy heads turned up in an eagle's nest! "There were supposedly five of them taken from an eagle's nest in the 1930s or thereabouts."[19] The University of Wyoming's collection includes the pygmy head that once belonged to Richard Phelps,[20] which is actually made from "plant fiber (a little turnip or potato head)."[21] These carved vegetables might have been made to sell as authentic mummy heads, with the story about the eagle's nest invented to give the impression that pygmies had been carried off and devoured by birds. This suggests the person who carved them was familiar with the local folklore about little people and eagles (see "The Little People" below).

It might seem odd that all of Wyoming's mummies should turn up in the 1930s. The idea that prospectors and miners could both find mummies in similar caves at the same time and in the same area is unlikely, but it is not impossible. 1932 was one of the worst years of the Great Depression. With one out of four workers unemployed, and hundreds of thousands wandering the country in search of jobs, people found themselves doing unexpected things to make money. Main and Carr might have taken up prospecting for lack of normal employment and found the mummy because they were looking in places more experienced prospectors ignored. (Harold Kirkemo wrote in "Prospecting for Gold in the United States" that "The lack of outstanding success in spite of the great increase in prospecting during the depression in the 1930s confirms the opinion of those most familiar with the occurrence of gold and the development of gold mining districts that the best chances of success lie in systematic studies of known productive areas rather than in efforts to discover gold in hitherto unproductive areas."[22])

Likewise, the miners might have been searching the caves for Indian artifacts they could sell. Perhaps Skinny Rimmer gave Mr. Cardwell the mummy because he thought it was interesting, but not easy to dispose of, like pottery or beads. (The manufacturing of mummy heads suggests there was a local market for them. Rimmer was from Hanna and may not have known this.) That Henry Cardwell left the mummy at the morticians suggests he did not think it was valuable either. If so, they both failed to see its money-making potential.

The Sideshow

The thread of the story gets lost for a while, but someone owned and displayed Pedro. Several witnesses recall seeing him or a mummy like him. One in particular noted: "The first time was in 1938 or 1939 in Casper, WY. It was in a trailer house . . . A 4th of July celebration or maybe the annual Natrona County Fair was going on at the time. The line into the trailer was very long. As I remember, it took about a 1/2 hour to get up to the trailer. Admission was 25 [cents]. The mummy was sitting on a table in the trailer and there was a guard at each end of the table—both armed. The line moved right along and I didn't have much time to look the mummy over."[23]

There are also rumors that Pedro toured colleges on the West Coast, being shown in a station wagon.[24] This stage of the mummy's career seems to have ended in Meeteetse, in northwest Wyoming, when it came into the possession of drugstore owner Floyd Jones. He may have bought it from whomever was showing the mummy in the trailer, but like everything else associated with Pedro, there's a story attached that ". . . two men had come into the bar or drugstore and offered to sell the little fellow. The druggist paid $2000.00 for the mummy and put it in a case on display in his store. The men blew the money on booze, food and women and didn't have a dime left of it."[25]

Mr. Harvey Wilkins, of the Big Horn Historical Society, remembers seeing Pedro at this time: "He [Mr. Wilkins] played basketball in 1945 in high school in Burlington, Wyoming. One evening, when they were to play Meeteetse, Wyoming, about 25 miles away, the coach arranged something for the whole team to get to do. They got to see the strange little dried up man in the drugstore in Meeteetse. By the door in the store was a case with the little dried man. He was about 45 [sic] inches high, the skin was still on it and the features were very plain to see. Someone or something has bashed him over the head and killed him and the blood had run down over his face and dried there."[26]

According to Floyd Jones' widow, Ida, Pedro was displayed in the drugstore and in Casper and Denver. Jones finally sold it for several thousand dollars in the mid-1940s, and its new owner, Ivan Goodman, made the mummy into more than a local curiosity.

It's Educational! It's Scientific!

Ivan P. Goodman was a natural born salesman, one of Casper's most aggressive used-car dealers,[27] a successful insurance agent, an unsuccessful candidate for mayor, and a collector. In addition to Pedro, he is said to have owned a pygmy head[28] and "a large ruby cut in a design said to be in vogue two centuries ago. Mr. Goodman believed this ruby to be one of the original crown jewels of France . . ."[29] Pedro and Goodman may have been fated to find each other.

Not long after the mummy's discovery in 1932, an article entitled "Origin of Mummy Remains a Mystery" appeared in the *Casper Tribune-Herald*. Directly underneath it was another called "Cars Derailed on Union Pacific Line," which informs us that "Ivan P. Goodman of Casper was an eyewitness to the crash. 'It was a perfect train wreck if such a thing were possible . . .'"

Goodman displayed the mummy in his office at the used-car lot. Lee Underbrink, a retired business man in Casper, still remembers that Al Tyler of Pittsburgh Paints and Glass made a glass case to

display it,[30] but Pedro seems to have spent most of his time in a bell jar on the desk. Some of the most detailed and controversial descriptions of Pedro date from this period and now may be a good time to take a closer look at the mummy itself.

He was six and a half inches tall sitting cross-legged and would have stood between fourteen and sixteen inches in height. Caroline Crachami, the "Sicilian Fairy," was one of the smallest people to ever live and stood just under twenty inches tall (she is believed to have been nine or ten years old when she died). Pedro's weight was around twelve ounces. His skin is described as bronze-colored, having a bronze-like hue, or simply, brown, and it was very wrinkled. He sat tailor-fashion with the arms crossed across the legs and the hands resting on opposite knees. It is not a relaxed position.

The top of Pedro's head was flattened, uneven, and appeared injured (some have even described it as gelatinous looking), with several sources mentioning a fringe of gray hair that is difficult to make out in the photographs. The forehead was low, with a broad flat nose, and a wide mouth that tilted just enough to give him a slight smirk. What most impressed those who actually saw Pedro, however, was the eyes, which "seem to peer at you distinctly." (The fact that the eyes survived drying out at all is surprising.)

George Hebbert has fond memories of the Goodman family and remembers being shown the mummy. Fifty years later, he is still struck by the way the eyes "stared at you. It made you uncomfortable . . . that right eye would look at you in strange ways." Mr. Hebbert also remembers the mummy having fingernails and toenails, but acknowledges that many years have gone by and won't swear to all the details. (He flatly denies there being any blood on its face.) Ivan Goodman also showed him something surprising that happened when Pedro was held under a reading lamp; the little figure would begin to "sweat" a liquid that George Hebbert believes was some kind of preserving fluid.[31]

The strangest description of the mummy comes from Robert E. David, who claimed that Pedro was "covered with a blonde fuzz" and had "canine teeth." These "canine teeth" suggest a traditional sideshow attraction called the "Devil Baby," which is a dried, infant-sized corpse, usually fake, with fangs, horns, and claws that is normally displayed inside a miniature coffin. There is a photograph of Mr. David holding a bell jar with what appears to be Pedro inside, so he probably had a close look, but no one else saw canine teeth (we will get back to this). The "blonde fuzz" is more complicated.

There is no obvious fuzz on Pedro in the photographs, but the earliest newspaper reports mention a "form of hair over its body."[32] The presence of body hair is key to the question of whether these were the remains of an infant or a mature man. (No mention is made of Pedro's genitals but there must have been some evidence he was male.) If the mummy was once covered with fuzz, it raises another possibility: that one of his owners removed it from everywhere but the pubic area to make the mummy look like an adult. Marco Polo describes seeing something similar done on the island of Sumatra near the end of the thirteenth century, when artificial pygmies were manufactured for export.

"You must know that in this island there is a kind of very small monkey with a face like a man's. They take these monkeys and by means of a certain ointment, remove all their hairs except around their genitals . . ."

Marco Polo describes the procedure in detail, ending: "Then they put these beasts out to dry, and shape them, daubing them with camphor and other things, until they look as if they had been men. But it is a great cheat . . . For such tiny men as these appear to have never been in India or in any other more savage country."[33]

Also, as unlikely as blonde hair might seem, it will come up again.

Whatever the details, Ivan Goodman was not content with simply owning the strangest paperweight in Wyoming and began taking Pedro to museums around the country.

Little Mummy, Big City

How exactly did a used-car salesman from Casper convince the Curator of the Department of Anthropology of the American

Detail of Pedro. (Wyoming State Archive)

Museum of Natural History in New York to become involved with a former roadside attraction? Goodman knew about selling, but he was fortunate that Dr. Harry Lionel Shapiro was interested in the relationship between environment and human stature. If Pedro turned out to be a genuine North American pygmy, it would be important to his work.

The Museum of Natural History and Dr. Shapiro had the mummy for about one week, during which time the little figure was X-rayed and examined by a physician. From March 3 to March 8, 1950, listeners to the Sunoco "Three Star Extra" radio show could follow the mummy's progress through these "cloistered laboratories" with commentary and interviews by host Ray Henley:

"I have just talked with Dr. Shapiro. Is the creature real . . . or fake[sic]. To all outward appearances . . . it seems real . . . the skin is mummified in a realistic manner. The features of the legs and body look too real for comfort to the mind.

"And when samples of the creature's hair were tested—the report came back: Human hair!

"Then the creature was placed under the X-ray machines—and to the consternation of some persons . . . the X-rays showed that there was a skeleton inside.

"But to the trained eye of Dr. Shapiro . . . these X-rays also revealed some contradictory evidence.

"Some of the bone structure is anything but human in its arrangement. The eye sockets are not the type found in mummies [see "Anencephaly" section]. The X-ray indicates there are no wrist bones between the one arm and hand which could be photographed.[34]

"So far, however, no examination has been made of the little man's hide . . . to see if it is human skin . . . there's been fear of damaging the specimen."[35]

Henley apparently arranged for the next examination at the "celebrated Chicago Natural History Museum . . . popularly known as the Field Museum," which according to Cecil Main already had the mummy in its collection. Pedro was X-rayed again—the transcript suggests that Sunoco "Three Star Extra" was not satisfied with the first results—and studied for one day by Dr. Paul Martin, chief curator of the Anthropology Department, and a group of experts. These included the curator for vertebrate anatomy, a zoologist, an archeologist specializing in "ancient methods for preparing human bodies for burial," and three anthropologists. On March 8, Dr. Martin announced their conclusions over the air.

"Henley: And are you prepared to say what your finding is?

"Dr. Martin: Yes we are, Mr. Henle [sic]. It is an Anencephalic Anemoly [sic].

"Henle [sic]: And that in everyday language is?

"Dr. Martin: It means an infant born without the top of its skull.

"Henle [sic]: Are those things common in human nature?

"Dr. Martin: No, fortunately not. They are known to the medical world but occur very rarely."

They go on to discuss the question of mummification. Dr. Martin explains that, "It was not mummified, but has all the outward appearances of being mummified" because "it happened to be deposited in a dry cave in a dry climate. We know from experience that human bodies laid away in caves are preserved for thousands of years."

Dr. Martin, however did not believe that Pedro was ancient.

"Henle [sic]: However, I notice in the formal statement of your findings that the Pedro Mummy is not a prehistoric miniature man.

"Dr. Martin: That is absolutely correct."

The formal statement says that, "X-rays show conclusively that the supposed 'dwarf' cannot be an adult. The development of the bones is exactly like that of a child at birth." (There is no mention made of a missing wrist bone.)

Concerning Pedro's age, the scientists felt that he was ". . . deposited probably not more than 25 years ago [around 1925]. Suggestions that it is the body of a miniature prehistoric man are fantastic. It might have been a 'skeleton' from someone's family closet, probably surreptitiously deposited in the cave in which it was discovered."[36]

The question of whether Pedro was an anencephalic infant or

an adult pygmy seemed to be answered, but the X-rays created more controversy. Some believe these showed "canine" teeth and related it to legends of the pygmy's taste for human meat (see "The Little People" below). Others saw what they considered fully developed molars, but since the mouth was closed, they could not be checked.

In addition to possible teeth, the skeleton may have shown signs of injury (fractures of the spine and collarbone) and these have been presented as evidence that Pedro was an adult member of a group that considered it shameful to die a natural death. Injuries, however, do not answer the question of whether he was an infant or a pygmy, and it is just as likely that an anencephalic child was the victim of infanticide. None of the scientists mentioned seeing pubic hair or fuzz.

At the height of Pedro's celebrity, Goodman had a hoopla flyer printed up entitled *It's Educational! It's Scientific!* that promised the mummy ". . . will amaze and thrill you. It's a pygmy preserved as it actually lived!" This flyer included four photographs, two X-rays, a brief history of the mummy's discovery, and comments from scientists. According to the text, the Anthropology Department at Harvard said Pedro was rare, and the curator of the Egyptian department of Boston Museum said it resembled Egyptian specimens. One of the most widely repeated comments came from "Dr. Henry Fairfield, noted scientist, [who] calls the creature *Hesperopithecus* after a form of anthropoid, which roamed the North American continent in the middle of the Pliocene period. All of them say it is the most perfect, prehistoric mummy ever discovered."

The Field Museum's actual opinion was very different concerning Pedro's age and there was no one named Dr. Henry Fairfield involved in examining the mummy.

In 1922, the noted palaeontologist Dr. Henry Fairfield *Osborn* identified a fossilized tooth found in Nebraska as belonging to a primate and christened it *Hesperopithecus haroldcookii* after the discoverer, Harold Cook. More fossil hunting between 1925 and 1927, however, showed that the tooth came from an ancient peccary. The error was acknowledged and Dr. Osborn remained one of the most important and respected scientists in the United States, dying in 1935, fifteen years before the mummy arrived in New York. (Also, the flyer gives the "two prospectors'" version of Pedro's discovery, while Henry Cardwell positively identified it as the mummy given to him by the miners. To complete the confusion, when Goodman died, his obituary included something closer to the "Mexican sheepherder" version of the story.)

Pedro is also supposed to have appeared in the newspaper column "Ripley's Believe It or Not," but the Ripley company has no record of this.[37]

The Mummy Vanishes

Ivan P. Goodman died after surgery for a brain tumor on November 11, 1951, in Denver, Colorado. His funeral was arranged by Gay and Horstman, the same place Henry Cardwell left his mummy, and it was around this time that Pedro vanished. There are several different versions of what happened:

1. Goodman had been feeling weak for some time before his death. According to his son, Dixon, he collapsed in the apartment of a "con-artist" in New York City who stole the mummy.[38]
2. An unnamed professor at Columbia University borrowed the mummy and never returned it. This points the finger at Dr. Shapiro, who was an adjunct professor at Columbia University from 1945 to 1970. It also recalls Mrs. Cardwell's story of the Wyoming professor who did not return the mummy.
3. A curator of a New York museum disappeared with the mummy in his possession. This also suggests Harry Shapiro, though he never disappeared before his death in 1990.
4. Someone named Leonard Waller or Wadler either bought or stole Pedro. Nothing more is known about him or his connection with Ivan Goodman. Was he perhaps the New York "con-artist"?

5. Robert B. David's article states that Goodman's widow, Helen, still had the mummy. This appears in the caption of a photograph showing the author holding Pedro inside the bell jar. Bashor's list of sources includes this article, and says it was published in 1962, but no one else has suggested that the Goodman family had the mummy at that late date. Perhaps an editor unfamiliar with the story was responsible for the caption.

6. In an article published in 1982, Guy Goodman, Ivan's grandson, expressed the belief that Pedro was in Florida.

It would be interesting to learn if Pedro's theft was reported to the police in Casper and New York City, or if the mummy was insured. (Goodman had been in the insurance business.) Both would require the filing of formal papers and, if the theft was not reported, why not?

Pedro's history ends in 1951 but interest in Wyoming's pygmy mummies has continued. People that become involved in the subject tend to fall into two camps: those who believe that the mummified remains of anencephalic infants are responsible for the belief in pygmies, and those who see the bodies and legends as evidence that a pygmy race did, or does, exist.

Anencephaly

Anencephaly is the "absence of cerebrum and cerebellum with absence of the flat bones of the skull."[39] It occurs during the third or fourth weeks of pregnancy, when the "cephalic," or head end of the fetus' neural tube, fails to close and the brain, scalp, and spinal cord do not develop properly.[40] Anencephalic infants are normally still born or "born dying,"[41] and while the brain stem allows their heart to beat and lungs to breathe, they are usually unconscious and senseless.

The disorder creates striking physical defects that are consistent with the mummy. Compare the flattened, "injured," and "gelatinous" appearance of Pedro's head with the anencephalic who has "a large defect in the vault of the skull, . . . meninges, and scalp [that] exposes a soft . . . mass of neural tissue covered with a thin membrane continuous with the skin." His prominent eyes can also be explained because "the optic globes may protrude due to inadequately-formed bony orbits."[42] The cause of anencephaly is unknown but it may be due to a lack of folic acid, vitamin B9, in the mother's diet.

Some discussions of the mummy say that anencephaly makes a newborn look old, but it would be more accurate to say that the reduced size of the head gives it seemingly adult proportions, while the drying out produced wrinkles. There is, however, another very rare disease called progeria (Hutchinson-Gilford progeria syndrome) that causes the symptoms and appearance of decrepitude in children; even rarer is "neonatal progeria" that causes something like old age in fetuses. Conceivably, the results could be an elderly looking infant, though this is unlikely.[43] Barry Strang, owner of the Wooden Rifle Ranch where Pedro may have been found, mentioned another interesting explanation for the mummy's appearance. He asked me if I had heard anything about the mummy being found with a little bag around his neck. I had not.

"Some people," he explained, "say the Indians wore little bags of uranium around their neck as amulets and that the radiation from it caused babies to be born like the Pedro mummy."[44] There is no mention of the mummies being found with objects of any description, and while this may be folklore, it's another aspect of the story worth looking into. Wyoming received fallout from nuclear testing in Nevada and it may be that anxiety about radiation-induced birth defects has become attached to the mummies.[45]

The Little People

According to one writer, Frank Carr exclaimed upon seeing Pedro, "By golly, Cecil! Darn if it ain't one of those pint-sized devils the Arapaho and Shoshone Indian know about—or the mummy of one."[46] Sarah Emilia Olden's book, *Shoshone Folk Lore*, includes a chapter on the Little People of Wyoming that expands on Carr's alleged statement and tells us more about them and their ways:

"The Shoshone Indians, before they were limited to the Wind River reservation, lived many, many years ago, all through this region. It was then inhabited by a race of pigmies or nimerigars . . . The Arapahoes said they were of very low mentality . . . They were child-like and irresponsible, but remarkably gifted in qualities which enabled them to subsist under very unfavorable conditions. The pigmies were stealthy stalkers and great fighters too. The shots fired by these little people, with poisoned arrows and unerring aim, meant sure death, and picked off the intruding Shoshone rapidly. The Arapahoes say they were also cannibals. They even hunted them down, carried them to their houses hewn out of rocks in the deep canyons, and ate them. To this day the houses of these pigmies can be seen in the depths of the mountains, and many of their skeletons have been found.

"The Shoshones say they . . . were clad in goatskins and always carried a great quiver of arrows over their backs [pygmies are credited with making the tiny arrowheads known as 'bird points.'] Not so very long ago a Shoshone actually held one . . . he saw one of the little people being mercilessly attacked by an eagle. The Shoshone clambered over the rocks and drove the eagle away. The little fellow expressed deep gratitude, telling the Shoshone he had saved his life."[47]

With the exception of this particular pygmy, the locals seemed to be in a situation similar to those who ". . . daren't go a-hunting, For fear of little men . . ."[48] Eventually the nimerigars became so troublesome that the Arapahos decided to destroy them. They drove them into a canyon with no exit, set fire to the brush, and the pygmies perished.

A number of native legends describe races of Little People in the United States. The Penobscot Indians of Maine believed in the *wanagemeswak*, which were fantastically ugly and something like paper cutouts, being ". . . so thin that they can only be seen in profile; a full forward look at them shows nothing."[49] Hawaii's nocturnal *menehune* were great builders, and in Minnesota, Ojibwa rock art often depicts little men called the *maymaygwayshi* who lived on the cliffs, and were associated with visions and shamanism.[50]

There are many more examples, though some people may not

accept their reality. In Wyoming, "many believe that the 'Little People' still exist. This is especially true of the Arapahoe and Shoshoni people but also among many whites in the Pedro Mt./Casper area. It is one of our most intriguing and persistent legends and, in Wyoming, it's bigger than bigfoot."[51]

After Pedro

There were no new developments in the history of miniature mummies until 1979. That was the year Dr. George Gill, a physical anthropologist at the University of Wyoming, saw pictures of the X-rays that had been taken of Pedro when he was at the American Museum of Natural History twenty-nine years earlier. He wrote to Dr. Shapiro and they agreed that the mummy was probably the remains of an infant with anencephaly.

Dr. Gill speculated that people might have lived in the Pedro Mountain area who suffered a high incidence of the disorder, and that the discovery of anencephalic mummies probably contributed to strongly held local beliefs in Little People. No mummies had been discovered since the 1930s, though, and apart from an occasional newspaper article, the story seemed over.

Then television got involved. *Unsolved Mysteries*, a series about strange phenomena, aired an episode about Pedro that included comments from Dr. Gill. Not long after that, something very unexpected happened.

"After I appeared on the *Unsolved Mysteries* program in 1994," Dr. Gill wrote, "a member of an old Wyoming family brought me a small female mummy that had been in the family for five generations. They thought it was the same as Pedro . . . and it was. It is perfectly mummified like Pedro, slightly smaller, sitting in the same unusual sitting position and has the same adult-like proportions." There are more tools available now than there were in 1950, and Dr. Gill was able to give this unnamed girl "DNA analysis, a radiocarbon date, and a complete 'check-up' at Denver Children's Hospital (pathology, genetics, etc.)." The owners, however, "only allowed our study to progress a day at a time (we never had the mummy in our possession overnight)."

The family has asked to remain anonymous so they're not available to be interviewed, but they believe a sheepherder found it (perhaps Señor Martinez?) in or near the Pedro Mountains in 1929.[52] "Like Pedro it seems to represent an anencephalic human infant who died during or before the normal birth process could occur."[53]

I asked Dr. Gill if the mummy might be affected by the Native American Graves Protection and Repatriation Act (NAGPRA)? Congress passed the act in 1990 so that Native American relics and human remains inside federally funded collections would be returned to their tribes of origin, or to culturally affiliated groups. Since the mummy is privately owned, I didn't think NAGPRA would apply, but Dr. Gill's answer was a surprise.

"Since we will probably never know the original land status of the find, and in light of the number of years that the family has had the mummy, I doubt that it will ever be claimed under NAGPRA. *We are not even completely sure that the little mummy is Native American (e.g. light blond hair, somewhat ambiguous DNA, etc.)*" [my italics].

We won't know what "ambiguous" means until the full report is published, but there's no indication it's a pygmy. "Like Pedro, it seems to represent an anencephalic human infant who died during or before the normal birth process could occur."

This second mummy may have also cleared up one of the biggest questions about Pedro; did he have adult teeth?

"Regarding that old tale about the adult teeth," Dr. Gill wrote, "they must have ascertained this through X-rays. It is my suspicion that the people interpreting the X-rays were not sure of what they were seeing. When we examined the X-rays of the little female mummy, it looked like she had a full set of teeth. In her case the mouth was open and we could plainly see that she had no erupted teeth. Apparently what we were seeing radiographically were the tooth buds of unerupted deciduous (baby) teeth."

Dr. Gill has his own list of questions. Why were the infants buried in such an unusual position? Was there an unusually high frequency of anencephaly in Wyoming at one time, and, if so, did it impact the people in some special way spiritually?

On the Trail of the Little Men

If Cecil Main was telling the truth, Pedro's cave was in the Pedro Mountains near the Pathfinder Reservoir and close to the town of Leo. Can it be found again? Its dimensions are known (four feet by three feet and fifteen feet deep), there should be enough small stones scattered around the entrance to seal it, and there should be evidence of old blasting nearby.

Most people believe it is on or around a gray mountain on the Wooden Rifle Ranch. Mr. Lee Underbrink of Casper writes: "The location of the cave has always been explained to me as Sec 23 of the Seminoe Dam NE quad sheet 7.5min. I have never been up there but there is a faint two-track road leading up to the place I have been told is the Little Man Cave."[54] (If you decide to go looking for Pedro's cave, get permission from the landowner.)

The Little Man Mine is nearby, but this was a working mine, not a natural feature, and no one has suggested that Pedro was found there.

The question of pygmies also needs to be explored. How widespread and strongly held are these beliefs? Are they based on personal experiences or folklore? Have there been sightings? Have people found footprints? What about those pygmy houses said to be "hewn out of rocks in the deep canyons"?

There is something interesting going on in Wyoming, something waiting for someone to look into it.

Addendum to Pygmy Enigma

In early 2005, I received a letter from Nancy Anderson at the Hanna Basin Museum concerning the "miners'" version of Pedro's discovery and the origin of the Little Man Mine.

She wrote: "Having recently consulted with the daughter of John 'Skinny' Rimmer . . . concerning his role in the mummy affair . . . Mary recounted that her father, Alex Pascoe, and Eric Lepponen discovered the Little Man Mine in 1954. The Union Pacific Coal Company closed the Hanna Mines in the spring of that year and converted their locomotives to oil. These men, having lost their jobs, joined the prospectors looking for uranium. They staked a claim in the Pedro Mountains and named it after the mummy which had been found there. Mary states that she had heard of that 'Little Man' but that if her father had been involved in his original discovery, the family would have known about it. Perhaps 1954 became 1934 and the mine became the mummy in your source? ['Pedro Mountain's Mystery Munchkin'] The other circumstances seem to fit your description very well."

This could, in fact, explain how "Skinny" Rimmer and the unemployed miners from Hanna became incorporated into the legend.

There are good reasons for thinking Henry Cardwell once had a mummy in his possession, but where did it come from? Eugene Bashor knew Mr. Cardwell and asked him about it: "Henry Cardwell was a close-mouthed man. When I asked him about the mummy, all he would say was that he had one once but that he had let it get away from him. When I asked him where he got it, he said, 'In Pathfinder Dam [sic],' but according to Bob Cardwell, Henry's son, it was found in a cave in a canyon leading down into the reservoir West and North of the old Parks place ranchhouse (still standing but unoccupied). Bob Cardwell says the cave may be underwater when the lake is full."[55]

While the origin and fate of Henry Cardwell's mummy remains a mystery, it appears that at least one of the riddles surrounding Pedro has been solved. There are a few hundred left, but it's a start.

6

A HORROR IN THE HEIGHTS

Baltimore, Maryland, 1951

*Short colorful specters like Detroit's infamous Nain Rouge
("Red Dwarf") are not unknown, but the classic phantom is
a long-legged figure in black.*

It wasn't easy getting a good night's sleep in the summer of 1951, but it was especially difficult for the residents of O'Donnell Heights, a housing project in southwestern Baltimore.

Americans were preoccupied with the threat of communism, Stalin's arsenal was growing more formidable, and while U.S. troops were fighting the Red Chinese in Korea, communist sympathizers and fellow travelers at home posed a danger from within. Mrs. Mary Markward, a secret agent for the FBI, testified before the House Un-American Activities Committee that communists were planning to "get the Baltimore steel workers following the party line, then get the trade unions too, [then] they would have the steel industry in the palm of their hands . . ." Undermining Baltimore's steel industry, the committee learned, was Bolshevism's "No. 1 goal."[1]

The weather that summer did nothing to soothe nervous

Baltimoreans. The city sweltered under a series of heat waves, and Philco air-conditioners ("easy terms, 65 weeks to pay") were not seen in neighborhoods like O'Donnell Heights, where steel mill and shipyard workers lived with their families. For them, tropical heat, Reds under the beds, and the real possibility of hydrogen bombs falling out of the sky were less pressing problems, however, than the specter in their streets.

Sometime in July, a tall, thin figure dressed in black began sprinting across the rooftops of O'Donnell Heights. It leaped on and off buildings, broke into houses, grabbed people, enticed a girl to crawl under a car, and played music in the graveyard. Groups of young men patrolled the streets, while many others sat by their windows at night, keeping a bleary-eyed watch for the "Phantom Prowler" that eluded pursuers and took refuge in nearby cemeteries. By the end of the month, police were arresting people for disorderly conduct and carrying weapons, but the gadabout phantom had disappeared and was never seen or, at least reported, again.

Things That Go Jump in the Night

O'Donnell Heights was only eight years old when the uncanny stranger made its appearance. Built as a housing project for defense workers at Bethlehem Steel, Martin Aircraft, and Edgewood Arsenal in 1943, it was not meant to be either beautiful or durable, and it wasn't. Tightly spaced, two-story row houses went up on sixty-six acres of what had been farmland, a brickyard belonging to the Baltimore Brick Company, and part of St. Stanislaus Kostka Cemetery.[2]

There are several burial grounds in the area: Evangelical Trinity Lutheran Congregational Cemetery, Mount Carmel, St. Matthew's, and the Oheb Shalom Congregation Cemetery, but the phantom showed a definite preference for St. Stanislaus and often appeared in the streets nearby.

By the time local newspapers noticed that something peculiar was happening in the Heights, the panic was almost over. Most of what we know about it comes from the back pages of Baltimore's two rival papers, *The Sun* and *The Evening Sun*, which printed a handful of articles on the phantom between July 25 and 27, when the sightings finally ceased. Reporters approached it as a typical "silly season" item and wrote the stories in tongue-in-cheek style, with *The Sun* including cartoon illustrations. No one seemed to know exactly when strange things started happening, but on July 24, Mrs. Agnes Martin told a reporter that the phantom had been seen "for the last two or three weeks."

The first incident that can be assigned a definite date took place on July 19. There was a full moon and temperatures were in the comparatively comfortable low seventies at 1 AM when William Buskirk, age twenty, ran into the phantom.

"'I was walking along the 1100 block Travers way [sic] with several of my buddies when I saw him on a roof,' related Mr. Buskirk . . . 'He jumped off the roof and we chased him down into the graveyard' . . . 'He sure is an athlete,' said one of the other boys. 'You should have seen him go over that fence—just like a cat.' (the [sic] fence bordering the graveyard in question is about 6 feet tall and trimmed with barbed wire along the top.)"[3]

The witnesses don't name the cemetery, but Travers Way is near St. Stanislaus.

Hazel Jenkins claimed that the phantom grabbed her some time that same week. She saw it twice at close-range (possibly in the company of Myrtle Ellen, though Ellen might have seen the phantom independently; the article's not clear), or Hazel may have been grabbed when the phantom tried breaking into the Jenkins' home (again, unclear.) Her brother Randolph Jenkins saw it soon after.

"'I saw him two nights after he tried to break into our house . . . He was just beginning to climb up on the roof of the Community Building. We chased him all the way to Graveyard Hill.' (The Community Building is the tallest structure in the project and at night is completely empty.)"[4]

The phantom next visited the family of Melvin Hensler, breaking into their house on July 20, but stealing nothing. After this unnerving experience, the family went to stay with Mr. Hensler's

The Phantom of O'Donnell Heights. (K.L. Keppler)

brother, but Mrs. Hensler returned to the house the next day and found a "potato bag left on the ironing board," which she thought belonged to the intruder. Mr. Hensler was so exhausted from staying awake that his eyes ached and he had started talking in his sleep.

Storms on the twenty-third lowered the temperature, and the phantom may have appreciated a break in the heat wave because it was especially busy on the night of July 24. *The Evening Sun* reported: "At 11:30 PM officers Robert Clark and Edward Powell were called to the O'Donnell Heights area where they were greeted by some 200 people who said they had seen the oft-reported 'phantom.'

"Clark said they pointed to the roof tops and someone yelled: 'The phantom's there!'"[5]

The police drove around and arrested a twenty-year-old sailor for carrying a hammer. He was fined five dollars.

A reporter from *The Sun* discovered thirty or forty people of all ages congregating at the back stoop of 1211 Gusryan Street, waiting for morning. He interviewed William Buskirk, Mrs. Melvin Hensler, and others who shared rumors and described their personal experiences. (The reporter also learned that Mr. Charles Pittinger was standing guard nearby with a loaded shotgun.) Jack Cromwell claimed the phantom lived in the graveyard, and Lynn Griffith of Wellsbach Way, which is adjacent to St. Stanislaus, told a story that suggested the prowler had talents that went beyond high-jumping: "One night I heard someone playing the organ in that chapel up there. It was about 1 o'clock."[6]

The phantom was also reportedly seen beckoning to Esther Martin from underneath an automobile and saying, "Come here, little girl."

Mrs. Ruth Proffitt's son saw it "at one place at the same time another person was seeing him somewhere else. He couldn't be both places at once, unless he had wings."[7] There were reports that the phantom leaped on and off twenty-foot-tall buildings, but Regina Martin was not impressed. "We kids used to jump off these roofs all the time," she said.[8] A fourteen-year-old girl offered to climb onto the roof and demonstrate, till someone reminded her about Mr. Pittinger and his twelve-gauge.

George Cook had mixed feelings about what was happening. He did not deny the reports of the phantom, just the possibility that something extraordinary was involved. In the end, he blamed the media.

"It's ridiculous to believe that . . . a man can jump from that height and not leave a mark on the ground. Yet this character does it all the time.

"It's my idea that when this thing is cleared up . . . it'll turn out to be one of these young hoodlums who has got the idea from the movies or the so-called funny papers, and is trying to act it out. This sort of thing appeals to detective story readers who are mainly looking for excitement."[9]

At 1:30 in the morning of July 25, Sgt. Emmanuel Sandler and other officers were called to an unidentified cemetery and arrested five boys, four of them teenagers, on charges of disorderly conduct. Around 10 PM that night, Patrolmen Elmer Powell and Milton Arczynski arrested Charles Kyle, Donald Keyser, and Edward Williams, all sixteen years old, on an embankment near the cemetery. Their six companions fled. Police responded to a call at 11 PM from a resident who reported footsteps on his roof, but nothing was found.

At some point during the day, Mrs. Mildred Galines heard the sound of someone trying to break into her house and ran outside barefoot, screaming, "It's the phantom!" It was actually police breaking down the door to serve a search-and-seizure warrant and the episode ended with Mrs. Galines and four male companions arrested on bookmaking charges.[10]

On July 26, the three young men who'd been arrested the night before—Kyle, Keyser, and Williams—were brought before Eastern Police Court Magistrate Emil Mallek on charges of disorderly conduct. They said they had been in the cemetery to help capture the phantom, and Mallek gave them a lecture and a fine of ten dollars each, suspended. "If you were older," he said, "I'd send you to jail."[11]

Newspaper coverage of the phantom was now exclusively humorous:

"In broad daylight a housewife heard a knock-knock-knock on her door followed by a stentorian voice proclaiming:

"'I'm the phantom, let me in!'

"Recovering almost immediately she said she peeked to see what he looked like. It was, she reported, only her insurance man, a fellow of limitless wit."[12]

That evening, the phantom was seen standing uncharacteristically still on the roof of a building at the intersection of O'Donnell and Gusryan Streets, the Graceland Park–O'Donnell Heights Elementary School. Patrolman Henry Roth investigated and saw that it was a ventilation pipe. Officers spent several hours that night following up sightings, including a report that the phantom was seen leaping into a yard where a particularly ferocious German Shepherd lived.

"The dog was found undisturbed by the visit. If the phantom had really landed, police conceded, he was resting, finger nails, cape and nimble toes, all in the stomach of the beast.

"'I ain't losing no sleep over this,' announced the dog's owner."[13]

The "Phantom Zone" was quiet after midnight.

On July 27, *The Evening Sun* announced that there had been no more reports, but "Police think he might be a teenager." The phantom may have gone, but the heat was back, with high humidity and temperatures in the mid-nineties.

Like most bizarre flaps, there was no satisfying resolution to the panic created by the Phantom of O'Donnell Heights. An unofficial version claims that armed residents finally chased it into the cemetery, where the phantom leaped into a crypt (or "sarcophagus") and vanished for good.

The Sun told another story:

"Four blocks from the fear area, in a bar where tippling offered fresh courage, men had a better explanation [for where the phantom had gone].

"'The Phantom,' claimed one patron, 'has moved to Highlandtown.'

"'Highlandtown!' another roared. 'Lord help the poor phantom!'"[14]

This anecdote has been repeated so often that its origin as a joke was forgotten, and some sources now report the phantom was last seen heading for Highlandtown, a neighborhood north of O'Donnell Heights.

Descriptions of the phantom were fairly consistent, considering that the encounters were brief, took place in the dark, and the figure was usually moving at speed. William Buskirk said, "He was a tall thin man dressed all in black. It kind of looked like he had a cape around him." (The phantom must have been thin to be confused with a ventilation pipe.) The only one who mentioned its face was Myrtle Ellen, who said it was horrible. She also agreed about the dark costume. The newspapers described the phantom as "black robed," suggesting long, loose-flowing clothes. Myrtle Ellen added that "He walks like a drape and runs like a horse."[15]

This comparison made more sense in 1951 when "drapes" were a recent memory. They were mainly young, black, and Hispanic men who dressed in a flashy outfit called a "zoot suit." In his novel *Invisible Man*, Ralph Ellison describes "drapes" in motion, which may give us some idea of what Ellen meant: "What about these three boys, coming now along the platform, tall and slender, walking with swinging shoulders . . . walking slowly, their shoulders swaying, their legs swinging from their hips . . ."[16]

Mrs. Melvin Hensler, discoverer of the sinister potato sack, saw the phantom three times and said that during one of these sightings it looked like it had a hump on its back.

Later descriptions of the phantom include the standard fiendish red eyes, but none of the eyewitnesses mentioned them. That detail seems to have been added when it became part of Baltimore folklore.

Speculation

Social scientists might describe events in O'Donnell Heights as an example of an "imaginary community threat." This approach suggests that the nine hundred families living there experienced "feelings of danger persisting within a diffuse population, lasting anywhere from a few weeks to several months . . . [the] creation and spread of these imaginary forces are a result of rumor and sensationalistic media reports that cause a conformity of misperceptions."[17]

Misperceptions certainly played a part, but they don't explain the relatively straightforward experiences described by William Buskirk and other witnesses. (I tried contacting William Buskirk, but he died in 1997. His sister-in-law told me he had a great sense of humor and while that might suggest a hoax, she also said that in the forty-six years they were related, William never mentioned the phantom. In fact, she hadn't even heard about the incident until I contacted her.[18]) The police never denied that people were seeing something, but like George Cook, they thought it would turn out to be a "young hoodlum." If it was, he was never caught, exposed, or confessed.

The story must have been spread by word-of-mouth because the two local newspapers ran just six articles, two of them fillers, and these appeared as the panic ended. The only one of these that might be described as "sensationalistic" was printed in *The Sun* on July 25, 1951, and included the experiences described by Buskirk, Mrs. Melvin Hensler, Jack Cromwell, and others. It ended on this sober, socially scientific, note: "The question of the prowler of O'Donnell Heights . . . continued to be not one of the phantoms, but of real people reacting to (and possibly creating) the unknown with their imaginations."

Some will take the phantom's affinity for St. Stanislaus as evidence that it was a ghost. Part of O'Donnell Heights was built on land that once belonged to St. Stanislaus, and the cemetery contains unmarked graves from the influenza epidemic of 1918. Also, bodies were dug up and reinterred when Boston Street was extended in the 1930s, but it's hard to see why any of this would stir up a spirit in July 1951.[19] No one suggested that the phantom was a vampire either, despite wearing a cape, that "most evocative of garments" representing "concealment, darkness, the secrets and terrors of the night itself."[20] Its alleged disappearance into a crypt, however, could indicate a different kind of subterranean connection.

Wm. Michael Mott, author of *Caverns, Cauldrons, and Concealed Creatures*, suggests that entities like the Phantom of O'Donnell Heights are flesh and blood beings that live underground. This may explain both their agility and their talent for making quick disappearances. "An origin or habitat in a region of higher pressure," he argues, "might result in a higher physical and muscular density in a life-form or being. This would equate to greater physical strength, the ability to make prodigious leaps and bounds, and a ruggedness of physiology not normally associated with those common-place creatures which have evolved or are designed to inhabit the surface of the earth."[21]

Other less corporeal possibilities are that the phantom was a psycho-physical thoughtform (see "The Bye Bye Man") or an "ultraterrestrial." These are a class of beings proposed by author John Keel, who suggests that inhabitants from a different part of the spectrum can appear in ours and cause mischief. Another possibility is demons, and there are in fact devils specifically assigned to the raising of "uproars" like the panic in O'Donnell Heights. Elementals are another possibility, one of the "lares, genii, fauns, satyrs, wood-nymphs, foliots, fairies, Robin Goodfellows [or] trolli" from traditional folklore.[22] Goblins belong in this category and there is a fictional version of them that recalls Baltimore's bouncing nuisance.

Charles Dickens' novel *The Pickwick Papers* contains several short stories, including "The Goblins Who Stole a Sexton." These are long-legged beings that appear in a cemetery on Christmas Eve to torment a gleefully misanthropic sexton named Gabriel Grub, who is digging a grave ("A coffin at Christmas! A Christmas Box. Ho! ho! ho!"). He is busy with the spade when goblins appear all around him.

"The first goblin was a most astonishing leaper, and none of the others could come near him; even in the extremity of his terror the sexton could not help observing, that while his friends were content to leap over the common-sized gravestones, the first one took the family vaults, iron railings and all, with as much ease as if they had been so many street-posts."[23]

Grub did not undergo a Scrooge-like conversion at the end of the story, but vanished and was never seen again.

Another possibility is that the phantom was a "monster" in the classical sense, a divine warning of impending misfortune. West Virginia's now famous "Mothman" is an example of a monster associated with disaster. Mothman was a red-eyed, winged humanoid that flew after cars and peeked into the windows of isolated houses. It haunted the area around the town of Point Pleasant where, on December 15, 1967, the Silver Bridge collapsed into the Ohio River, leaving forty-six people dead. The creature disappeared around the same time and has become more or less linked to the accident. Today, after several books and a feature film, a statue of Mothman stands in downtown Point Pleasant—the monster has been turned into a mascot.

O'Donnell Heights had a less dramatic fate. The neighborhood simply decayed, eaten away by poverty, crime, and neglect.

As for the phantom, it has not been sighted in Baltimore since 1951. The story, however, is revived every Halloween when newspapers print the annual roundup of local ghosts, legends, and haunted houses.

More Ectoplasmic Ectomorphs

There have been other specter-inspired panics in the United States. In September 1944, for example, Mattoon, Illinois, was the site of a two-week scare similar to the one seen in O'Donnell Heights.

It was caused by a lanky figure in black called the "Mad Gasser" that sprayed paralyzing gas into peoples' homes, but did not make fantastic jumps when chased; it just ran away and was never caught. (For a thorough account of the Mad Gasser, see Chapter 20, "The Mad Gasser of Mattoon and His Kin," in Loren Coleman's *Mysterious America*, Paraview Press, 2001.) The Gasser is often cited as a classic example of "mass hysteria," but like Gloucester in 1692, this mass hysteria left behind physical evidence, including footprints (apparently made by a pair of woman's high-heeled shoes), a cloth soaked in noxious chemicals, a skeleton key, and a lipstick tube. Though the Gasser was something like the Phantom, Baltimore's goblin more closely resembled the terror of Victorian England known as Springheel Jack.

Like its Yankee cousin, Springheel Jack was tall, thin, and hideous.

It made superhuman leaps over walls, ran across rooftops, and easily outdistanced pursuers, but it was not necessarily considered a supernatural creature. The people of nineteenth century Britain were accustomed to miraculous technology and credited its phenomenal jumping to shoes fitted with metal springs. In other respects, Jack was a far more colorful proposition than anything seen in O'Donnell Heights: a fire-breathing gargoyle with clawed hands and pointed ears that wore a cloak and a tight-fitting suit of either metallic mesh or white oilskin (cloth made waterproof with oil). It had a silver helmet on its head, and to complete the ensemble, a lantern strapped to its chest. It was something of a hybrid, a medieval bogey using modern techniques to frighten people out late. Its bizarre exploits eventually became part of popular culture, and Jack appeared as a character on the stage and in several "penny dreadfuls," the inexpensive and overwrought serial novels that were enormously popular during the period. In spite of all this exposure, or possibly because of it, Springheel Jack inspired panics all over England between 1837 and 1877.

The appearance of long-legged phantoms seems to breed a fear out of all proportion to the danger they represent. If, for example, every accusation made against the Phantom of O'Donnell Heights were true, it would have been guilty of trespassing, disturbing the peace, disorderly conduct, housebreaking, and making suspicious advances towards a little girl (assuming Esther Martin was a child; her age is not mentioned). This is not the kind of crime wave that normally inspires city residents to form armed patrols or keep dawn to dusk vigils, but there's no predicting how human beings will react to the unusual.

The appearance of a Springheel Jack–type figure in the town of Mineral Point, Wisconsin, for example, did not produce a panic. Richard D. Hendricks, the premier chronicler of Badger State oddities, has looked into the case and generously contributed the following account of the Mineral Point Vampire:

"On March 30, 1981, while on a routine patrol, police officer Jon Pepper saw a caped figure lurking in a cemetery. The cop described the person as 6' 5", but he was seeing him in the dark, and estimated this based on tombstone height.

"'He didn't have makeup on his eyes or mouth and he had short hair,' Pepper said. 'It was one of the weirdest things I've ever seen in my life. I don't know if he was on drugs, a mental case, or if someone was playing a joke. I've never seen anyone that tall before in Mineral Point.'" He gave chase, but lost his prey as the "vampire" jumped over a four-foot barbed wire fence and disappeared into a cow pasture. Pepper was a fairly young officer at the time and he took a good deal of ribbing. "It was a two-day wonder, with lots of media coverage. I've gone through newspapers for months after the event, however, and nothing else was reported. The town had a field day with it, and 'vampires' showed up in advertisements and drink specials, but alas, no new vampire."

Hendricks continues: "Subsequently, I have heard some speculation that it was an actor, playing a role. Mineral Point is an arts community, and the well-known American Players Theatre is located in nearby Spring Green. I've recently heard from a second person that the event may have been a prank—a bit of theater to prank a prankster. Pepper himself was well known in Mineral Point as a prankster. I found an article that mentioned he sometimes wore a gorilla costume to scare people. Recently I learned the names of some people who may have been involved; I have yet to chase them down.

"I haven't made up my mind, but I am leaning toward a prank that went further than anyone expected. It happened the evening of March 30—the day before April Fool's Eve. The graveyard chase also happened the same day that President Reagan was shot. A vampire flapping around a cemetery may have been a coincidental well-timed arrival of a bit of levity the media could use to take the public's mind off this near tragic event."[24]

Panics, however, are not a thing of the past. As recently as February and March 2005, Santa Fe, Argentina, was terrorized by *el Loco Tejado*, "the Rooftop Madman." Detailed accounts have not appeared in English, but the story sounds familiar. A tall figure (two meters, or six feet, six inches tall) in a black cape, was scaling high walls and leaping from rooftop to rooftop, while frightened citizens locked themselves in at night, or patrolled the streets with clubs and machetes. The sheriff described it as an outbreak of "generalized psychosis" or "mass hysteria."[25]

Mass hysteria is a reasonable explanation. It's also reasonable to wonder why, when mass hysteria can take so many forms, that it often arrives as a tall, high-jumping man in black?

7

THE LOST BOYS

Newark, New Jersey, 1978

This is the story of a mass disappearance.
There's no reason to believe it was paranormal, but somehow that
makes it worse; when it's paranormal you don't expect a solution.

A *turnepike* was once a "revolving barrier furnished with spikes used to block a road."[1] Today, the term applies to any highway with a tollgate unless it's referring to *the* Turnpike, in which case it means the New Jersey Turnpike—that twelve-lane ribbon of concrete stretching 148 miles across the state from Deepwater in the southwest to West New York in the northeast. The Turnpike is the busiest road on planet Earth and the most memorable part of it, certainly the one that makes the strongest impression, is the passage through the industrial corridor of Essex County.

Here it snakes through the kind of landscape that Soviet Five-Year planners used to dream about: a panorama of smokestacks, pipelines, electrical pylons, swooping concrete highways, iron bridges, and rail yards stretching from one horizon to the other. Vast machines of production and commerce dominate the scenery. There are chemical plants and petroleum refineries, fire-breathing towers and columns of smoke that hang over tank farms swollen with petrochemicals. Massive steel gantries, like stick-figure horses, stand in rows along the docks, moving mountains of cargo containers between ships, trucks, and railroad flatcars, while airplanes pass overhead with metronomic regularity.

As you travel past old factory towns and through the stink of crude oil being cooked into gasoline, you come to a spot where the gritty sprawl is interrupted by skyscrapers. This is Newark, the largest city in New Jersey, and home to a quarter million people.

Newark has a bad reputation, but a stroll through the downtown may change your mind. Broad Street is lined with discount stores and crowded with shoppers, while companies like Prudential Insurance, Bell Atlantic of New Jersey, and PSEG have their offices in the towers overhead. There are fine Art Deco and Beaux Arts buildings, an excellent museum, and a dome on top of City Hall that glitters like a gold skullcap. The impressive New Jersey Performing Arts Center is nearby, along with a new sports arena. Behind these showpieces, however, is the old Newark.

It is a bleak, dangerous city of razor wire, vacant lots, rubble, and rotting housing projects whose residents live in conditions rarely seen in twenty-first-century America.[2] This Newark has one of the highest infant mortality rates in the country, unemployment that is twice the national average, and a significant number of citizens who live in poverty. The crime, drug abuse, and HIV/AIDS rates are equally grim.

This didn't happen overnight. Newark's decline began as long ago as the 1930s or 1940s and hit bottom in July 1967, when a series of riots left the city in flames, twenty-six people dead, thousands under arrest, and ten million dollars' worth of property destroyed. A thousand businesses were looted or burned, many never to reopen, and middle-class white residents vanished into the surrounding suburbs. Newark remains the most segregated American city outside of the Midwest, with a population that is predominantly black and Latino.[3]

In the January 1975 issue of *Harper's Magazine*, an article titled

"The Worst American City," by Arthur M. Louis, ranked America's fifty largest cities. It used twenty-four categories, including crime, health care, income, parkland, etc. and determined that "The city of Newark stands without serious challenge as the worst of all. It ranked among the worst five cities in no fewer than nineteen of the twenty-four categories, and it was dead last in nine of them." Louis concluded that "Newark, is a city that desperately needs help."

It looked as though it was a city with nothing left to lose. Then on a summer night in 1978, five young men vanished and it managed to lose a little more.

The account that follows is based primarily on articles that appeared in the Newark *Star-Ledger* and *The Times of Trenton* between 1978 and 2000. Newark police officials did not respond to requests for clarification or information, so much of what appears here is qualified with "allegedlies" and "apparentlies."

An Otherwise Ordinary Day

Things were different in 1978. A peanut farmer was President of the United States; you listened to music on a radio, an eight-track tape, or a vinyl record ("Three Times a Lady" by the Commodores was number one); and the only way to walk down the street while talking on a phone was with a very long cord.

August 19 was sunny and hot. Temperatures reached the upper eighties that afternoon when five friends met at West Side Park to play basketball. They were all young black men: Ernest Taylor, aged seventeen; Randy Johnson, sixteen; Melvin Pittman, seventeen; Alvin Turner, sixteen; and Michael McDowell, sixteen. All of them lived in Newark, except McDowell, who was from East Orange. Whether or not they actually played basketball is unclear—like most of the events of that day, the details are uncertain.

At some point they met Lee Evans. Evans was twenty-five years old, a carpenter, and presumably a sizable presence (his nickname was "Big Man") who the boys knew personally or by reputation. He sometimes hired teenagers to do odd jobs and enlisted all five to help him move boxes in nearby Irvington.

Evans may have wanted to start right away, but there was a change of plans; he was driving a pickup truck and dropped off some of the boys at 8 PM, so three of them had dinner at home that evening. An hour later, two young men were seen in the truck (a witness thought one of them was McDowell.) They may have been heading towards East Orange, because sometime between 9:30 and 10:00, McDowell stopped at home to change his clothes and get a drink of water. His mother saw another person in the truck (presumably, this means sitting in the flatbed; Evans would have been in the cab), but she could not see who it was.

Irvington, East Orange, and Newark are adjoining cities, and the Big Man seems to have spent much of that Saturday driving from one to the other with the boys in tow. By 10:30, he had picked up all five, but "by that time, he decided it was too late to move the boxes and drove around in the truck before dropping the kids off at Clinton Avenue and Fabyan Place [in Newark] at 11 PM."[4] They all

Corner of Clinton and Fabyan in Newark, New Jersey. (Robert Schneck)

lived close by on Leslie Street, Beverly Street, Hawthorne Avenue, and Clinton; perhaps McDowell was planning to spend the night with one of his friends before going home.

After Evans dropped the boys off, "There was a 20–40-minute period when they were seen apart," said Detective Charles Conte, "two of them together, then three of them together."[5]

Today the intersection of Clinton and Fabyan probably looks much the same as it did then. There are small shops, a Laundromat, and a liquor store on the ground floor of a two-story apartment building. A bus stop is there, and a handsome brick building that's been boarded up with trompe l'oeil curtained windows. The streets surrounding it are lined with old oversized wooden houses, some well maintained, others dilapidated, that sit uncomfortably close together. Many have porches on every floor, and on a hot Saturday night in August, residents must use them. There must have been open windows and people talking on their front steps that night, but even with all these potential witnesses, the boys vanished like ghosts sometime after 11:40 PM.

The Investigation

Witnesses apparently saw the boys up to the last few minutes of the night of August 19, but not the morning of the twentieth or afterward. If they disappeared on the twentieth, the next important event happened on Monday the twenty-first when one of the families received a collect call from Washington, D.C. The caller did not identify himself but said, "Your brother and his friends were caught in a truck heist and are being held in the Washington youth house."[6] Published accounts do not say who received this call or how they responded.

Missing persons reports were filed but there was nothing remarkable about them as individual cases. It was only when "the reports were compiled, four by Newark police, one by East Orange police, that authorities realized that their disappearances could be linked . . ."[7] (The police department was experiencing a severe manpower shortage in 1978. This may explain why the disappearances were not linked sooner.[8]) Since the case involved juveniles, it was apparently the responsibility of Community and Youth Services, and in October Det. Charles Conte was assigned to "oversee and consolidate" the investigation. Like several other detectives, "Chuck" Conte would remain involved in the case for the rest of his career and into retirement. (Conte joined the force in 1966 and made detective in 1970. He worked in several different units including the Youth Aid Bureau and Homicide, and received numerous medals and commendations, including one for saving children from a burning building.) A friend who knew him in 1978 wrote, "I remember when he started investigating the case and how it kept him up at night . . . I also know that the case bothered him until the day he died."[9]

Private citizens also became involved. The "residents of the Clinton Hill section circulated fliers throughout the area and neighboring states, offering a $1,500 reward for any information on the whereabouts of the teens. A Montclair based organization, called the Crisis Coalition, organized search parties and also circulated fliers throughout the state."[10] In addition, when "a community group demanded the case get attention, the city formed a task force, the prosecutor formed an investigative team and a local citizens group mobilized."[11]

The "Big Man," Lee Evans, found himself a suspect. He was questioned several times and different theories were constructed around him, but Evans passed a polygraph test, presumably had an alibi, and was never charged. (December 1978, however, was an especially bad time to be hiring teenage boys who subsequently disappeared. That month the bodies of twenty-eight young men and boys were found under the house of Chicago contractor John Wayne Gacy, who was also known for employing them.) No other suspects have been publicly named.

Police in Newark canvassed the neighborhoods, while the boys' friends and relatives were interviewed and their rooms searched for clues. It turned out that some had marijuana and a history of minor run-ins with the law, but there was no reason to believe they were involved in the kind of crime that might end in mass murder. These were, after all, kids who moved boxes for pocket money, and the police did not suggest that their disappearance was the result of a "drug deal gone sour." Instead, they kept looking.

The boys had not joined the military or been put in jail. They had not been admitted to a hospital or mental asylum, or run off and joined the circus. (This might sound improbably Norman Rockwell-ish, but traveling circuses do hire unskilled laborers called "roustabouts" to do the least glamorous jobs.) Police also checked political groups and religious cults; by November their investigation had reached the jungles of Guyana.

That was the month that the Rev. Jim Jones, charismatic leader of the People's Temple, ordered his followers to commit "an act of revolutionary suicide protesting the conditions of an inhumane world."[12] Over nine hundred people died in Jonestown, and New Jersey police went through the lists of casualties to make sure the missing boys were not among them.

Detectives did this whenever a number of young black men turned up murdered. They sifted through the victims of the Atlanta child killings in 1979–1981 and those of Jeffrey Dahmer in 1991.

High profile cases like these, however, were exceptional, and most of the investigation consisted of following up leads that led nowhere. The call from Washington, D.C., was one of the few real clues investigators had, and while the caller was never found, the telephone was traced to the National Visitor's Center. This was a vast granite railroad terminal, the former Union Station, but by 1978 it was a decaying and largely deserted tourist attraction that soon closed.[13] While police and civilians kept searching, the families suffered the pain peculiar to those whose loved ones are missing.

Time passed. By the fifth year citizens' groups had done what they could and faded away. In 1986, detectives were following up a tip supplied by a psychic, the first of three occasions acknowledged by officials. Otherwise, the search for the boys had almost ceased to generate new clues.

The years rolled into decades and the case remained the responsibility of Community and Youth Services, even though the "boys" would now have been around thirty years old. It remained a missing persons case as it "cannot officially be handled as a homicide probe because no bodies have been found."[14]

In 1991, Everett L. Hairston was the only detective working on the case full time, and it fascinated him. He made sure every lead was followed up and called the disappearances "the most intriguing case I've ever worked on.

"It's not often," he added, "that you find absolutely no physical evidence regarding a disappearance."[15] Not to mention a quintuple disappearance.

Psychic Interlude

Psychic phenomenon may seem out of place in law enforcement but police can be among those most likely to trust instinct and hunches. They are also pragmatists whose main interest is results, and many of them are willing to try unconventional methods to get those results (a 1993 survey showed that 37 percent of urban police departments have tried psychics[16]). This approach, however, is usually pursued with discretion or off the official clock because there are members of the public who strongly object to dallying with what they consider the occult. Debunkers and religious fundamentalists are among the most vocal, with the former believing that psychic powers do not exist and are therefore a waste of taxpayers' money, and the latter crediting demons with supplying the psychic's information (who may, in fact, be possessed), and no good can come of that. Neither group is bashful about expressing their opinions, but detectives in Newark were looking for five missing teenagers, with no clues and nothing to lose.

Several newspaper accounts mention that a Ouija board was used, but details are lacking and the first psychic used in the case has not been named. He or she lived in Irvington and suggested that police investigate a garbage-covered lot south of Newark International

Airport. In 1986, an abandoned oil tank was excavated but no traces of the boys were found, and it was ten years before police publicly pursued another extrasensory tip.

The tip came from the best known (and certainly best liked) of all the psychic detectives who regularly worked with police, Dorothy Allison. It's difficult to say how many cases Allison has been involved with, but she claimed thousands and was probably not exaggerating. (My mother knew a local detective who consulted her many times.) Allison's home in suburban Nutley, New Jersey, was stuffed with hats, badges, and citations presented to her by different police departments, and detectives even went on record with some of her successes. Nutley detective Salvatore Lubertazzi was quoted in the July 1979 issue of *The Journal of Law Enforcement* as saying that "she's found twenty missing or deceased persons for us since 1968."[17]

Allison had a vision about the missing teenagers in 1979 and believed they had been murdered. The bodies were burned and what was left buried near the airport. Police did not act on this and filed it away; perhaps it was too different from theories they were working on at the time (possibly involving Lee Evans).

In 1994, detectives Armandina Tahaney and Angel Ramos of the Youth Aid Bureau began a two-year review of the case and presumably developed a scenario that agreed with Allison's. We can only guess what they thought but we do know what they did.

In the first week of May 1996, officers from the Newark Police department, the sheriff's department, and Conrail explored a weedy area near the airport with four German Shepherds from the Ramapo Search and Rescue Dog Association. They were searching "an overgrown lot beneath overpasses for Interstate 78 and Route 22 where the two roads run parallel north of the airport."[18] The dogs identified several possible grave sites, and police spent the next few days digging, discovering fragments of teeth, and bones that must have belonged to an animal because no more is heard of them. Two police chaplains were on hand in case bodies were found, and their presence, along with the time and money that went into the operation, suggest some confidence in its outcome. In the end this was another false trail, but the department was grateful for Allison's help and presented her with a plaque reading, "In appreciation for using extraordinary psychic ability to assist the Newark police in an ongoing investigation."[19]

A month later police would try again, this time with the help of John Monti, a Florida-based psychic who specializes in missing person cases. Monti had been interviewed on a New York City radio program in February, when host Kay Thompson, a former Newark resident, asked him about the missing boys. According to Thompson, "Retired cops and individuals who had worked on the case heard him and called up saying there was no way he could have possibly known the facts he did."[20] On June 5, 1996, two detectives escorted Monti around Newark and he identified several spots where bodies might be buried. As for the missing boys, Monti pointed to an "abandoned property" on Camden Street (which is near West Side Park, where they played basketball) and said, "There used to be a house here . . . All the boys were here alive that night and there was a fire. But only one of them is buried underground here."[21]

Nothing was found, however. Mere ESP was not going to solve this riddle.

Anniversary

The story of the boys' relatives will probably never be written. Expressions like "lack of closure" don't mean much when compared to a lifetime of loss, disappointed hopes, and the dreadful imaginings that haunt a sleepless night.

When the investigation began, police kept the families informed and the mothers called them regularly, but with no news, detectives phoned less often, and eventually the families "stopped bothering them."[22] Likewise, the five families grew close after the boys' disappearance but eventually lost touch. One of the mothers told reporters what so many people say when a loved one vanishes, that they would rather hear bad news than not know what happened.

By 1998, Ernest Taylor's and Michael McDowell's mothers had died, and the families of the other boys could not be located or preferred not to comment on the twentieth anniversary of the disappearances. Only the McDowells spoke to the media: "The family decided the best way to remember today's anniversary of Michael's disappearance was to aggressively remind people that his case is still unsolved, hoping publicity will spark a memory."[23]

Helen Simmons, Michael's aunt, spoke with a mixture of sadness and anger. She told reporters about dreams where the boys would come home and explain where they had been, and how she glanced at men on the street to see if they might be her nephew.[24] She blamed the police for not getting on the case sooner. "It's the 20th year and we just feel like nothing has been done . . . These children have not come home. I don't know if people really realize that."[25] (Simmons has suffered her own losses. In 1990 her daughter, McDowell's cousin, Joanne Cobbs, was found murdered in Branch Brook Park.)

The case file shows what has been done. It includes "42 pages of single-space type chronicling day-to-day events of the first two years of the investigation . . . [what Det. Hairston referred to as 'the Bible' of the case]. Its accompanying box of files, pictures, handwriting samples and scribbled notes attest to thousands of man-hours devoted to the case that failed to uncover anything but theories."[26]

Chuck Conte retired in 1997 but never stopped thinking about the disappearances. "It wasn't only my duty as a police officer to solve the case, it was my duty as a human being," Conte told reporters in 1998. "I've put my blood sweat and tears into this case: I want it solved."[27]

Detectives Tahaney and Hairston have also retired. Despite the lack of evidence and the passage of time, Hairston remained optimistic. "I know there is an answer to this mystery and one day the case will be solved."[28]

This was not just an empty hope. Some disappearances are explained, or possibly explained, years after they happen.

Genette Tate

The five boys in Newark were not the only ones to disappear on Saturday, August 19, 1978; it was a good day for vanishing. "The UK's Longest Running Missing Persons Case"[29] began on the same date in southwestern England.

Around 3:30 PM, thirteen-year-old Genette Tate was on her bicycle delivering newspapers outside the village of Aylesbeare in East Devon. Friends saw her pedaling along a country road called Within Lane, and a few minutes later, discovered her bicycle lying on the ground along with the newspapers, but Genette was not there.

Thousands of volunteers turned out to look for her. Colin Wilson, author of numerous books on crime and the paranormal, got the psychic Robert Cracknell involved in the search, but nothing was found. It was like she had evaporated. Years passed, the officers that originally handled the case retired, but the investigation continues and there have been important new developments. A sample of Tate's DNA was recently recovered from an article of clothing, which will make it possible to quickly identify any remains that are finally recovered. Police also suspect that a convicted serial killer named Robert Black may have been responsible.

Black has been found guilty of murdering three girls. He is suspected of having killed a half-dozen more, and there is evidence that he was in the area when Genette disappeared. (Black, incidentally, is not unlike Cracknell's psychic impression of the killer as a "laboring type, with a record of mental illness."[30]) He denies any involvement, but if a plausible case is built against him—even one that does not reach the threshold required for a conviction—it shows how a missing persons case that began the same day that the boys vanished can be resolved decades later. On the other hand, British police probably suspected someone like Robert Black from the beginning: a stranger who abducted and killed Tate then successfully disposed of the body. Detectives in Newark have no idea what happened; the only thing they seem confident about is that the boys are dead.

The Genette Tate case raises other questions. Overpowering a single thirteen-year-old girl who is fighting for her life is probably not easy, but it presents fewer difficulties than five teenaged boys aged sixteen and seventeen; how do you control them? And assuming they were murdered, what happened to the remains?

Speculation

Two things are certain: the boys' Social Security numbers have never been used and none of them have ever applied for driver's licenses. Almost everything else is speculation. Consider the phone call from Washington, D.C.; Everett Hairston thought this was "the most concrete lead in the case," and Chuck Conte felt it "could be an indicator of what really happened 20 years ago."[31]

" 'My question is, how did the caller know to say, "your brother" to the person who answered the telephone?' " Conte asked. The caller's choice of words also troubled Conte as unnatural, and he wondered if it was the boys themselves spinning a tale to explain their absence.

"No other juvenile detention facility in the country is called a youth house, only in Essex County."[32]

If Detective Conte is right and the boys were putting together a cover story, why would they say they had been arrested for stealing a truck? Teenagers aren't known for clear thinking, but what could be gained by saying they were involved in a felony? And, after receiving this news, wouldn't the family have contacted the D.C. police to find out what had happened? In 1991, Det. Hairston said that "you would have thought one of them would have called home,"[33] which suggests he didn't think they made the call, but if they didn't, who did?

Maybe one of the five knew someone in Washington, D.C., and asked him or her to phone his family. That would explain where the caller got the phone number and knew what the relationship was between the missing boy and the person who took the call. It may also be that they were killed and the killer or an accomplice made the call, but why? Was it an attempt to create a distraction? If so, where did they get the personal information? Did the boys make the call and die on the way home? Was one of them forced to phone home? How old was the sibling who received the call? Did he or she remember it accurately? There's no shortage of questions.

Judging by newspaper accounts, the investigation never focused on Washington, D.C. It was reported that "[Newark] Police checked with officials in the area and found no record of missing youths."[34] Of course, the boys weren't from there, so who would notice if they were gone and file reports? This is vague, and it's unclear what, if anything, the D.C. police did.

Did the boys vanish on purpose? After a long hot day of moving boxes and sitting in a truck, did they decide to take their money and make a big weekend of it? (This assumes that Lee Evans paid them; no account mentions this.) Helen Simmons denies the possibility of their running away, but teenagers have been known to take off without notice; maybe they left voluntarily and met with some misadventure along the way. Lillie Williams, the mother of Melvin Pittman, mentioned another possibility: "one popular theory has the five moving to Washington, D.C., and joining an underground religious sect."[35] She did not say she believed this.

Det. Hairston seemed less inclined to think they had been murdered. "In this case," he said, "all the boys did everything together, so you know—because there was a group of them—they probably weren't overcome."[36] Chuck Conte, on the other hand, suggested the possibility of "a group being responsible for the disappearance of the teenagers or killing them, but he is unsure of the motive."[37] What group could he have been referring to? A street gang? Something more formidable, like the Mafia, Hell's Angels, or Ku Klux Klan? Armed men could control five teenagers, but how such an encounter might have occurred is pure conjecture.

Dorothy Allison and John Monti both believed that the boys were killed and agreed that at least some of the bodies were in or around Newark. Allison said the remains were burned (Monti, or the newspaper accounts, is more vague and just mentions a fire) but if they are right, it raises other difficulties. Burning a human being is no small task.

A furnace is the best way to do it. Open fires, even in a pit, are difficult to hide. They attract attention, produce quantities of foul-smelling smoke, flare out of control, and take hours to do a thorough job. Teeth, bone, and hair fragments survive all but the most intense incineration, and internal organs are surprisingly durable.

In an article about spontaneous human combustion, Dr. Mark Benecke wrote: "The high temperatures of the outer parts of the burning body is not maintained internally, where fluids in the various organs and cavities help prevent their incineration . . . The effect is not commonly known, and even first-year medical students express surprise when shown burned corpses containing intact organs."[38] Five cadavers quintuples the job, and if the teenagers weighed as little as one hundred twenty pounds each, that would mean six hundred pounds of muscle, fat, blood, and bones would have to be destroyed. Even the most efficient modern cremation retorts (or "pathological incinerator") would require four hours to consume this amount.[39] There would also be five outfits, ten shoes, and personal effects to dispose of, like wallets and watches as well as zippers, eyelets, and buttons. None of these have ever been found or at least recognized as related to the disappearances.

Most likely, the remains would have been partially burned before being buried in a hole large enough to hold five bodies, but "Burial is hard in cities, and in the country the grave is readily distinguishable by traces of disturbed soil. Shallow graves give up their dead. Deep ones take hours to dig, and neighbours think it odd."[40] Then come the inevitable dog walkers and Boy Scouts who always seem to find the people that other people are trying to lose. If the bodies were dumped in the water, nothing has ever surfaced.

John Monti said that one of the boys was buried under a house, and private homes can make effective cemeteries. In 1915, the skeletons of six young men were discovered in shallow graves beneath the house of Eugene Butler, a North Dakota man who had died in an insane asylum two years earlier. Stella Williamson, an elderly church treasurer from Gallitzin, Pennsylvania, died in 1980, and left a letter directing police to a trunk containing the mummified bodies of five infants wrapped in newspapers. Even apartments can be turned into morgues; English necrophile John Reginald Halliday Christie squirreled away six corpses in a tiny London flat, putting one under the floor, three in the cupboard, and two out in the garden. There is a lot of construction underway in Newark, and it's possible that new evidence, even bodies, could turn up while digging new foundations.

It's hard to imagine a happy resolution to the disappearances but there are also less gruesome possibilities to consider. Could they have had some kind of accident? Chuck Conte discussed this in 1998: "They could have stolen a car and gone for a joy ride. Who knows, they could have cracked up on a back road, driven into a creek or lake, and sank."[41]

This sounds improbable and raises more questions. Was a car stolen in the vicinity of Clinton and Fabyan that night? Did any of the boys know how to drive? Presumably yes, or the truck heist story would make even less sense.

It also recalls urban legends about concealed car wrecks. These typically begin with a crew out doing roadwork, when someone drops a tool, and a metallic "clang" is heard coming from an unexpected place. They look inside a pile of boulders or clump of underbrush and discover a very old car that had crashed years before with the skeletons of the passengers still sitting in the seats.

Folklorist Jan Brunvand traces this story back to a tale collected in nineteenth-century Norway. It tells of a hunter in a remote valley who shoots an arrow at a bird, misses, and hears a metallic sound come ringing out of the trees. The arrow has struck a bell, and it leads him to a church that has been completely overgrown by forest. The building is all that remains of a town wiped out by the Black Death.[42]

Det. Conte, however, may have been remembering a more recent case, one that explained the disappearance of five Florida teenagers in 1979. They vanished as completely as the boys in Newark, and if Conte felt a little jealous, it only means that homicide detectives are human, too.

March 3, 1997
After 18 years, Missing Teens' Bodies Found in Submerged Van

BOCA RATON, Fla. (AP) - Matthew Henrich's mother started writing the letters to her son shortly after he disappeared nearly 18 years ago.

"Matt, I never know how to start. I don't know whatever happened to you or even if you are alive," said one of Peggy Kelly's missives.

"We all just keep praying to God that one day, you'll walk into the door. We have been doing everything we can to find out and always come up empty."

Ms. Kelly, 57, of Fort Lauderdale, sent the letters to the Social Security Administration, which promised to forward them to her son if he ever got a job and sent them a change of address.

But since July 14, 1979, it appears that Henrich's body and those of four other teen-agers were in his van, submerged upside down in a murky drainage canal, say Palm Beach County sheriff's deputies and relatives of the teens.

A fisherman spotted the crushed brownish-gold 1976 Dodge van last month just west of Florida's Turnpike. It was coated with algae and full of mud. A salvage yard manager preparing to demolish the van on Friday noticed bones in the mud and called the Palm Beach County Sheriff's Office.

Investigators found more bones, bits of clothing, jewelry, two soggy wallets, beer bottles, and a driver's license bearing the name of one of the five who vanished that night, said sheriff's spokesman Paul Miller.

The teens were identified as Kimberly Marie Barnes, 16, of Lake Forest; Phillip Joseph Pompi, 19, of North Miami; William R. Briscoe, 18, of Hollywood; and John Paul Simmons, 18, of Lake Forest; and Henrich, 18, of Miami Gardens.

Positive identification will take some time because the bones are intermingled and extremely decomposed, said Dr. John Thogmartin of the county medical examiner's office.

Missing person reports were filed for each of the teens but led nowhere. The van was never reported stolen or missing. Investigators say there's no indication of foul play.

"I never lost hope, but I suspected something was wrong," the twice-widowed Ms. Kelly told the Sun-Sentinel in Fort Lauderdale on Sunday. "In writing these letters, I had the impression I was communicating with my son even if I cried the whole time I wrote."

There were many rumors surrounding the teens' disappearance, including that they had been spotted in Huntington Beach, California. This prompted Lisa Zakovsky, Phillip's sister, to drive to California in 1979 where she spent 10 days searching for her brother.

"It was very hard for me because we were very, very close," Ms. Zakovsky said. "I'm glad to know that Phillip's been with God the last 17 years."

"It was easier to not know," a visibly upset Jamie Reffett, Kimberly's sister, said at the canal Sunday. "I could have lived with that the rest of my life."

Today

Nothing about the five boys has ever appeared in the National Crime Information Center or the National Center for Missing and Exploited Children. Most of the detectives who have worked on the case are retired or have passed away. Conte died of a heart attack in 2000, at the age of sixty, while lying on a beach in Costa Rica.[43] A detective remained assigned to the case, but with the weight of new cases and a lack of evidence, the disappearance couldn't be a high priority.

The case remained open but there were no new developments until March 2010, when Lee Evans was arrested for murder and arson. His cousin, Philander Hampton, reportedly told police that Evans had a dispute with the boys about drugs, so Hampton and Evans drove them to an abandoned house at gunpoint, locked the five teenagers inside, and burned it down.

This contradicts newspaper accounts of the boys' and Evans' movements and raises the possibility that authorities might have recovered physical evidence. As of October 2010, a trial appeared likely and, for the first time, a solution to the decades-old mystery seemed possible.

8

THE BYE BYE MAN

Wisconsin, 1990

*This story is different from all the others in this book.
First, the source is a close friend. Second, though this might sound
dramatic, readers who are genuinely frightened by the paranormal or
troubled by obsessive thoughts should consider skipping this chapter.*

"Sit opposite your partner and rest your fingers lightly on the glowing planchette. Now ask your question. Concentrate very hard . . . and watch as the answer is revealed in the message window. Will it tell you YES . . . or NO? Will it give you a NUMBER . . . or SPELL out the answer?

"Ask any question you want. Ouija will answer.

"It's only a game—isn't it?"

Those are the words printed on a Ouija board box.

Though it is packaged and sold as a game, the Ouija board was developed as an improved method of "communication between the material and spirit world."[1] Practitioners consult the boards for many reasons: to learn the future, find lost objects, or get advice, but its purpose is to talk with spirits, and it is spirits that are supposed to provide the answers. Whether this is actually what happens is a subject for debate, but it adds an element of mystery and danger to using the Ouija board that no other game can equal. You can play all the Parcheesi you want without having to worry about demonic possession, and if you throw Monopoly into a fire, it won't scream the way Ouija supposedly does.

Most people who use the board will have a harmless, slightly spooky, experience that they will enjoy. There are stories, however, of ghostly phenomena occuring when the board is used: strange raps, apparitions, pointers moving on their own and even spelling out threats. Many of these happen during slumber parties and are reported by pre-adolescent girls who have scared each other into hysterics. (Note the sample questions printed on the box: "Will I star in my own music video?" "Does Taylor like me?" The manufacturers know who's buying their product.) Older more sober witnesses have also had disturbing experiences and the subject of this chapter is an example of the latter. To put it into context, however, let's begin with the Ouija board itself.

O-U-I-J-A

The Ouija board comes in two pieces: the pointer, or "planchette" that moves, and the board that it moves across. The board is rectangular with a smooth surface and has the words "YES" and "NO" printed along the top, and the trademarked name "OUIJA, MYSTIFYING ORACLE" between them. The letters of the alphabet are arranged in two rows, followed by the numbers 0 to 9 and "GOOD BYE" at the bottom. The corners are decorated with black billowing clouds, a smiling sun, moon, star, and a séance scene.

The pointer is a heart-shaped platform with a porthole in the center. It sits on three short legs, and slides across the board choosing numbers or letters in response to questions. The letter that appears in the porthole is the one that's supposed to be chosen, though some people, or spirits, prefer using the pointed tip of the planchette.

There have been attempts to link Ouija with ancient forms of divination, but it was developed to meet the specific needs of nineteenth-century Spiritualism. Americans have been consulting spirits for a long time, using everything from ritual magic to bibliomancy, that is, divining with books. The Puritans, for example, practiced a form called "gospel cleromancy," in which the questioner puts on a blindfold, opens the Bible to a random page, places the point of a pin on the text and applies the verse to their situation (the Rev. Increase Mather denounced the custom). Methods that relied on sorcerers or Bible texts, however, were unequal to the needs of Victorians, who were long-winded on both the physical and astral planes.

Orators of the period were judged by their stamina, diaries and personal correspondence were voluminous, and it was not unusual for spirits to dictate full-length books or deliver lectures on everything from geology to metaphysics. Those who attended séances did not passively receive wisdom from the Other Side, they asked questions on every conceivable subject and this created a lot of traffic between the worlds. A medium made this manageable by summoning the spirits themselves, producing written messages or rapping out responses, but demand for their services was high, as were their fees. With only so many mediums available many Spiritualists relied on a technique called "table turning."

This was "the simplest and crudest form of communication . . . The usual procedure is to form a circle around the table, place hands lightly, with fingertips touching, on the leaf and, with lowered lights or in complete darkness, wait for manifestations . . . Apparently, there is an intelligence behind these movements. If the letters of the alphabet are called over in the dark the table, by tilting or knocking on the floor or tapping the sitter, indicates certain letters which connectedly spell out a message, often purporting to come from someone deceased."[2] A similar system appeared at Spiritualism's inception to communicate with the rapping poltergeist that was harassing the Fox family in Hydesville, New York, in 1848,[3] but this was not the first time that spirits rapped out responses to questions. Humbert de Birck, for example, died in Oppenheim in 1620, and strange noises were soon being heard inside his house. "The master of the house, suspecting that it was her [sic?] brother-in-law, said:

'If you are Humbert, tap on the wall three times.' Three taps were heard . . . not only at the wall, but also at the fountain."

Table turning was dull, time-consuming work; fifty-three letters have to be called out just to spell "hello," but this was an ingenious era, and ways of overcoming the bottleneck in communications were soon available.

In one technique, the medium moved her finger over an alphabet printed on a board and the spirits rapped when she touched the one it wanted. This was followed by mechanical devices, with names like the "Spiritscope" and "Pytho or the Thought Reader," that combined a printed alphabet with a sliding or revolving arrow and picked out letters without audible signals from Beyond. The planchette (French, "little plank") was invented as another tool for spirits to write out messages or draw pictures.

The original planchette was a small platform with three legs: two had rotating casters and the third was a pencil, inserted point down. The operator(s) rested their fingertips on top and waited for the spirits to start scribbling. Sometime around 1886, an unknown genius (possibly in Ohio) combined the planchette with an alphabet board and created the "talking board."[5]

Using one did not require special skills or talents, and with practice it became possible for sitters to receive message at a speed that approached conversation. The board worked so well that by 1886, "Its use and operation [had] taken the place of card parties."[6]

The $1.50 Miracle

The word "Ouija" made its first official appearance on February 3, 1891, in the *Patent Office Gazette*.[7] The boards were manufactured by Charles W. Kennard's, Kennard Novelty Company (price, $1.50), and then by the Ouija Novelty Company. In 1901, an employee of the second firm, William Fuld, was put in charge and became the most important man in the history of Ouija. In twenty-five years he would sell millions of boards and make it a household word.

"One of William Fuld's first public relations gimmicks, as master of his company, was to reinvent the history of the talking board. He said that he himself had invented the board and that the name Ouija was a fusion of the French word 'oui' for yes, and the German 'ja' for yes."[8] This doesn't make much sense, though, and leads to the question of what does "Ouija" really mean?

The Oxford English Dictionary repeats Fuld's explanation, but the online Museum of Talking Boards mentions another possibility. "Charles Kennard called the new board Ouija (pronounced wE-ja) after the Egyptian word for good luck. Ouija is not Egyptian for good luck but since the board reportedly told him it was during a session, the name stuck. Or so the story goes. It is more likely that the name came from the fabled Moroccan city Oujda (also spelled Ouijida and Oudjda). This makes sense given the period's fondness for Middle Eastern cities and the psychic miracles of the Fakirs."[9] Personally, I think there may be something to Kennard's story.

The Egyptians were great believers in amulets, and along with scarabs and ankhs, carried carved representations of the *Udjatti*,[10] the Eye of the Sun, and the Eye of the Moon. The *Udjat* or *Wedjat*-eye looks like the capital letter "R" with the upper half replaced by an eye; it "was a symbol of the power of the god of light used to drive away evil."[11] "Udjatti," "Udjat," and "Wedjat" all sound something like "Ouija," and the board is decorated with the "Eyes of Heaven," that is, the sun and moon. (On the other hand, the moon is a crescent and a star, a symbol of Islam, and point back to the Moroccan city as the original inspiration.)

Fuld died in 1927. He was supervising work being done on the roof of the Ouija board factory in Baltimore when an iron support gave way and he fell three stories to his death. The family continued to produce a variety of novelty boards until 1966, when Parker Brothers bought the company. The toy manufacturing giant still makes Ouija, and while modern boards are smaller, they glow in the dark, as does the lightweight plastic planchette.

And Yet It Moves!

There are two popular explanations for how the Ouija Board works. The first is based on a physical/mental phenomenon known as automatism.

Automatism is unconscious mental and physical activity which, in the case of Ouija boards, means the sitters are responsible for moving the planchette and producing the messages. What appears to be spirit communication is actually a conversation between different parts of the sitter's (or sitters') mind. The resulting material may be so alien to the participants' notion of themselves, however, that an external source seems to be responsible.

Ouija is a form of automatic writing, a phenomenon in which "the writer does not consciously know what he is writing: this is described as 'disassociation,' which means that there is some temporary separation of the part of the personality engaged in the writing process from the normal state of the individual."[12] At one time psychologists encouraged their patients to produce automatic writing as a way of gaining access to the subconscious; nevertheless spirits are often credited as being the true source of the material. One of the most famous, and prolific, examples of the phenomenon began on July 8, 1913, when Pearl Curran, a housewife in St. Louis, Missouri, allegedly received a message on her Ouija board saying, "Many moons ago I lived. Again I come. Patience Worth my name."

Worth claimed to be the spirit of a poor English woman who was born in Dorsetshire in 1649, and immigrated to the New World, where she was killed in an Indian massacre. Curran's education was limited, but the long "collaboration" between housewife and spirit produced millions of words in the form of historical novels, plays, poems, short stories, and a monthly magazine. Six of the books were published. ("Dr. Usher, Professor of history in Washington University considers *The Sorry Tale*, a composition of 350,000 words, 'the greatest story penned of the life and times of Christ since the Gospels were finished.'"[13])

Curran's work is considered well written and the historical details accurate, but it remains unclear how much of it came from the author's subconscious. According to the Museum of Talking Boards: "when push came to shove, Pearl Curran denied that the Ouija board was responsible for her prolific output. Many of her admirers refused to believe this, and maintained that Pearl had buckled under the pressures and criticisms from outsiders."[14]

A more popular explanation for how Ouija boards work is spirits. The board was designed to improve communications between the material plane (our world) and discarnate intelligences existing on the astral plane, a higher, less physical, world composed of finer material than this one. These beings include spirits of the dead, spirits that have never lived, angels, demons, and others. The medium, or sitters, serve as a point of contact between the planes, and communication occurs via telepathy ("mind-to-mind communication of thoughts, ideas, feelings, sensations, and mental images"[15]), or through a limited form of possession, in which case the experimenter(s) cedes some control of her body to the spirits.

These entities display a wide range of moral, intellectual, and emotional qualities that can present difficulties for the operators. Spirits must be relied on to identify themselves, and can claim to be anyone from Imhotep to the sitter's Aunt Emily. This allows lonely or mischievous spirits to indulge in masquerading and provides an opportunity for other, less innocent, beings to introduce themselves into the sitters' lives. It is this danger of consorting with demons in sheeps' clothing that inspires much of the criticism aimed at Ouija boards. (According to Ouija folklore, placing a pure silver coin on the board will keep evil spirits at bay, but don't rely on it.)

Edgar Cayce, Kentucky's famous "Sleeping Prophet," warned against automatic writing and is supposed to have called Ouija a "dangerous toy." While Cayce's quote hasn't been confirmed, the sentiment has, and other mystics share his opinion. (In 1968, the "*Psychic News*, a noted English spiritualist newspaper . . . began a campaign demanding a ban on the sale of ouija [sic] boards."[16] The harshest attacks, however, come from Christians who cite biblical prohibitions against divination and repeat lurid anecdotes about the board that recall anti-drug literature.

Ouija boards are presented as the occult equivalent to marijuana, a minor lapse in itself, but one that opens the door to more destructive behavior. "Most Ordinary People buy the game thinking that is [sic] would be COOL to talk to a spirit of a dead relative or a famous person."[17] Dabbling in the occult supposedly leads to witchcraft, then Satanism ("NOTICE HOW I PROGRESSED FROM BEING ENTERTAINED TO HAVING MY LIFE COMPLETELY WRAPPED UP IN THE OCCULT!" screams one website[18]), and ends in demonic possession and damnation. ("Please WARN as many as you can about the *Ouija* board. This dangerous occulic [sic] device not only can lead to demon possession, but even eternal damnation in the lake of fire."[19])

Demonic possession is presented as the natural outcome of consulting the board, though the most famous example is actually a work of fiction. William Peter Blatty's 1971 novel, *The Exorcist*, tells the story of Regan MacNeil, a girl who becomes possessed after meeting a demon named "Captain Howdy" through the Ouija board. The book and film are probably the best-known representations of demonic possession in popular culture, and the author claims he was inspired by a real case. It was reported in a newspaper story, "Priest Frees Mt. Rainier Boy Reported Held In Devil's Grip," that appeared in *The Washington Post* on August 20, 1949. The boy involved was supposed to have become possessed after experimenting with a Ouija board, but the account, including this detail, is poorly documented and unreliable.[20]

In addition to automatism and spirits, there are cases in which the experimenter appears to be in telepathic contact with living, incarnate minds, other than their own, but these are rare.

Astral Mischief

What spirits actually say varies from practical information about the location of the car keys to metaphysics, with many entities showing a particular interest in philosophy. Jane Roberts, for example, was using a Ouija board when she first contacted Seth, an "intelligence residing outside time and space." Roberts went on to channel Seth and published his teachings in a series of books. There is a darker side to these communications though, with some boards producing demented or obscene material, and others seemingly intent on frightening the sitters. Ouija boards have even been blamed for murder.

One scandalous episode of this type began on November 18, 1933, when Mattie Turley, aged fifteen, shot her father with both barrels of a twelve-gauge shotgun at their ranch near Springerville, Arizona. He died a month later and the girl was arrested along with her mother, Dorothea Irene Turley. Mattie told police a strange story. "The daughter confessed to the shooting, blaming her action on an ouija [sic] board, which she claims 'told me to kill daddy so that mother could marry the cowboy.'"[21]

Dorothea was a beauty contest winner from New York who had been educated in England and married Everett J. Turley, a retired Naval officer. They moved to Arizona for her health, and there she developed an interest in Ouija boards and a certain "handsome cowboy." According to the prosecution, Mrs. Turley convinced Mattie that spirits wanted the girl to kill her father and that she would not be punished for doing it.

The defense claimed that the shooting was an accident; that Mattie had been aiming at a skunk when she hit Mr. Turley, and police had forced her to confess. As for Dorothea, "She knew nothing of the Ouija board's instructions to her daughter and . . . the girl was 'talking insanely.'"[22]

Mrs. Turley was convicted and sentenced to ten to twenty-five years in the State Prison at Florence, where she served three years before the conviction was overturned. Mattie received six years in the State Reform School for Girls at Randolph, where "the little girl told the reform school matron that she was sorry she killed her father but that she was 'certain of the ouija [sic] board's instructions.'"[23]

Most people that experiment with the board will not end up in a cell or a ward or tied to a bed listening to the *Rituale Romanum*. Critics typically overstate dangers in the "Marijuana: Assassin of Youth" vein,[24] but that doesn't mean they don't exist. Sitters can become over involved with the board; it can leave them scared or emotionally upset, and paranormal phenomena have been reported in connection with Ouija.

The Bridge to Body Island incident is not one of those cases where the planchette flew through the air or spelled out B-E-E-L -Z-E-B-U-B, and while the horrors are gruesome—almost lunatic—they're never seen. In that respect it's something like W. W. Jacobs' famous short story, "The Monkey's Paw."

"Eli," one of the principles, wrote this account in third person form. I have changed the names and included some explanations.

The Bridge to Body Island

At the end of the summer of 1990, three friends living in a small town in Wisconsin carried out an experiment with a Ouija board that brought them into contact with a monster.

Sun Prairie is in the southern part of the state and is best known as the home of artist Georgia O'Keeffe. [She was a painter of big flowers and cow skulls; O'Keeffe hated Sun Prairie.] It is surrounded by dying family farms and scattered hamlets like Pumpkin Hollow and Killdeer Creek. It has some of the last one-room schoolhouses in this part of the country and, more importantly for this story, is just three miles from the railroad hub between Chicago and Minneapolis.

I had just received a B.A. in Cultural Anthropology from the University of Stevens Point-Wisconsin, and decided to pursue a graduate degree in Madison, Wisconsin. Katherine, my long-time girlfriend, was born and raised in Madison and was working there for the summer.

I got a job at a group home in Sun Prairie, working the night shift. It came with a small salary and a smaller apartment in the basement of the house. It was on the outskirts of Sun Prairie, a stone's throw from Pumpkin Hollow on a dead-end street near the county line. I was responsible for watching over three adults who had Prader-Willi syndrome (PWS), a genetic disorder named after two German doctors. People with PWS manifest a number of disturbing symptoms, including stunted growth, limited brain development, and high-pitched voices (like cartoon characters), but the most dramatic symptom is their insatiable appetites. PWS patients do not produce the hormones that inform the brain that the body has had enough to eat, so they always feel famished. Since the brain thinks it's starving, it sends messages to the endocrine system that stunt growth and preserve every calorie taken in. A vicious cycle develops, with the body squeezing every last bit of fat out of food while cannibalizing the muscles for more protein. As a result, those with PWS get obese with fewer calories than normal adults, and never feel full no matter how much they eat. In order to satisfy their ravenous appetite, patients will periodically try to escape, break into stores, order huge meals at restaurants, etc. They would eat anything, whole jars of mustard, toothpaste by the tube full, even medications if given a chance. My job was to keep them in the house and out of trouble in the evenings.

Katherine's parents and most of her friends had moved away and she was working part time for a political organization. Her job did not pay enough for her to live in the city, so she moved into the basement with me.

I drove to school every day and dropped off Katherine at work; then we rode back to the group home at night so I could work. Between school and the group home's evening schedule, we didn't have time to meet new people in the area, so we were very happy when a mutual friend moved there from Stevens Point. John got a job as a dishwasher and took a room in a nearby boarding house run by an old woman.

The three of us hung out all the time in Sun Prairie. We took walks in the fields, checked out the local graveyards (some of the oldest in the state), and collected local folk tales and urban legends. (I was studying both Anthropology and Folklore and previously had done parapsychology work with O.B.E.s at Stevens Point.) [An O.B.E. or "out-of-body-experience" is the sensation of having left the body. Spiritualists call it "astral projection" and it may or may not be paranormal in nature.]

That fall, a childhood friend gave me a Ouija board that he'd found in the attic. It was an old wooden board and John and I spent hours trying to get messages, but all we ended up with was gibberish. I convinced Katherine to join me at the board but our results were no better. Then she tried it with John and they immediately started to get results.

For the next few days, the three of us spent hours on the board. The messages came from the "Spirit of the Board," an entity that had never lived and that acted as an interlocutor between other entities and us. These entities had different personalities and individual ways of moving the planchette: some used abbreviations, some were terrible spellers, and others used Latinate words with some skill. Some preferred using the pointed end of the planchette to choose letters, while others liked the porthole.

The Spirit of the Board would control and introduce each of these intelligences, and for weeks we communicated with them. Like the Spirit of the Board, they claimed to not be spirits of the dead but some kinds of archetypes or free-ranging consciousnesses. Each entity had its own personality, but for the most part they concentrated on imparting New Age–type wisdom and philosophy. Since the board would only work when Katherine and John used it, I got the job of transcribing the proceedings and carefully filled notebooks full of the correspondences.

I am interested in scientific parapsychology and wanted to find out if some sort of paranormal phenomena was indeed happening, so I started to conduct a number of experiments with John and Katherine. They got messages from the board by touching the planchette with their palms or a single finger, with the Ouija board turned around, and wearing blindfolds in a darkened room while I followed the planchette with a flashlight. No matter what innovation I introduced, the results were the same; the entities kept communicating. I suggested automatic writing and even attached a small golf-pencil to the planchette but this did not work. Then we tried for EVP phenomena with similarly disappointing results. [EVP or Electronic Voice Phenomenon are the "spirit voices" caught on recording equipment, especially audiotape.] We also tried pendulums, but again the board was the only method that got results. I decided to add a new twist to the procedure by writing down the questions without saying them out loud. I selected questions that would need to be answered by numbers, words, or letters. Though the answers were vague, as usual, they remained consistent and could be said to correspond with the questions.

After weeks of this, John and I were getting bored with the eight or so entities that the Spirit of Board would let us communicate with and their repetitious philosophy. I was determined to talk to a spirit that had lived, whose existence could be verified, and who would give us information we could check. At one point the board told us that there were indeed other entities we could communicate with but they might be dangerous, and it encouraged us to continue talking to the other entities. After some digging, we heard about a sinister entity that wanted to communicate with them. They also found out that this entity was not only a human but was still alive. John and I were eager to communicate with whoever it was but Katherine was adamantly against it. She had a history of paranormal experiences and had been sufficiently spooked by them to not even watch scary movies; she certainly had no interest in deliberately contacting something sinister. Katherine refused for a few days, but the two of us were able to wear her down and she agreed to try again. She was not happy about it but was very close to both of us and we were determined to see it through.

At first, to Katherine's relief, the board simply refused to communicate with the desired entity and instead brought us the same old tiresome folks. The questions that I wrote or asked were now all about the living mind that wanted to reach us. At one point we learned that all of the other entities knew about this person and gave us a name; he was called the Bye-Bye Man. Upon seeing that name spelled out on the Ouija board, Katherine panicked and quit the board again. We tried to press on without her but nothing happened.

Katherine was now very clear; she refused to try to communicate with the Bye-Bye Man but we cobbled together a compromise. We would not communicate with the Bye-Bye Man directly but would try to get some piece of information about him from the other entities, something that could be tracked down and verified. Now we began interrogating the spirits but they refused to cooperate until John got an idea: we would stage a strike. The Spirit of the Board was given notice that we were tired of the entities and their refusal to tell us anything about the Bye-Bye Man, so from now on we were going to be using the Parker Brothers' board that we'd bought for the planchette.

We tried the new board for a few days but got nothing. Even Katherine and John got nothing useful. Still, we waited a few more days before picking up the old board and discovered that the strike had worked; when we communicated with the Spirit of the Board again it agreed to tell us about the Bye-Bye Man.

The story came out in bits and pieces over several sessions. It began in Louisiana sometime in the 1920s, when an odd little boy was put in an orphanage in Algiers. Nothing is known about his parents but the boy had albinism, a genetic condition that causes a lack of pigment in the eyes, skin, and hair; but it was his behavior that was strange. Maybe part of it was the physical and social isolation that can happen to children with albinism; their unusual appearance, the way they must avoid the sun and, in this case, ever worsening eyesight. He could not play games, and may have been teased or bullied by the other children.

As the boy grew older, his behavior grew worse, and there were run-ins with the people who ran the orphanage. Then one day he was arguing with the head nurse in her office when he attacked her with a pair of desk scissors, leaving her an invalid.

After this savage assault, he fled. He ran away to the train-yards, and began traveling around the country by jumping freights. The viciousness he'd already shown was now unleashed, and he began carrying out random killings. His eyesight finally failed, but that did not stop the Bye-Bye Man; he created a companion for himself, sewing together pieces of his victims into something named Gloomsinger.

Gloomsinger was made from tongues and eyes and endowed with some kind of life. It acted like a hunting dog, sighting the next victim and letting out a whistle only the Bye-Bye Man could hear, which brought him to the scene. In order to keep Gloomsinger in good repair though, it was necessary to sew on new eyes and tongues regularly. The Bye-Bye Man became something of an expert at removing them, and their removal identified his handiwork. The organs were kept (along with his other belongings) in a seaman's bag he called his Sack of Gore.

At some point, he also developed a kind of telepathy and was able to sense when people were talking, or even thinking, about him. As long as they thought about the name "Bye-Bye Man," they were psychic beacons and he was able to get a bead on them and slowly track them down. He would travel hundreds of miles by rail to attack unsuspecting gossips, and talk of the murders quickly spread through the rail-yards and hobo camps.

The board also gave us some other details. The Bye-Bye Man had long hair and a tattoo on his wrist; he wore glasses that were painted black and wore a wide brimmed hat that covered his white face and something that looked like a pea-coat. And he carried the Sack of Gore. We also got a magic recipe that would help the Bye-Bye Man find us. I don't remember the details, but we had to take a big green glass bottle, cork the mouth, and go out into the moonlight. Then if we quickly uncorked it and held it to our ears, we would be able to hear Gloomsinger whistling.

We also asked where the Bye-Bye Man was now. Chicago, the board said, and coming closer.

Katherine became very afraid, and refused to participate in any more sessions. I was not happy because I didn't think we'd gotten anything worth checking, and preliminary searches produced nothing. John, meanwhile, thought the whole thing had been very interesting.

It looked as though the experiment was over and the Ouija board was put away. Soon after that, Katherine began waking up in a panic; she had suffered panic attacks as a teenager, but they were back and they always seemed to hit at 3 AM, the "soul's midnight." [This refers to the idea that most deaths and suicides take place at 3 AM or between 3 and 4 AM. It would require a statistician to prove whether or not this is true, but the idea is certainly widespread. "My

The Bridge to Body Island in Wausau,
Wisconsin. (Robert Schneck)

Grandfather was in the Merchant Navy in WWII, and he said the worst watch to be on was 3–4 AM, because that's when your soul was supposed to be 'at its lowest' . . ."[25] "I remember my grandparents (both nurses) referring to 4 AM as 'Death Hour' or something like that, as it was the most common time for patients to die. They put this down to probably being in deepest sleep by that time, and that it's the coldest part of the night . . ."[26] "I can also state from personal experience of signing search warrants, that the police still like to raid drug dealers at 3–4 AM as they figure they will be at a low ebb then and less likely to put up resistance."[27]]

John's work schedule had changed so we saw less and less of him. Without the Ouija board experiments, the focus returned to normal pursuits like work and school. One day I ran into John at the Student Union at the college, so we had a beer and talked. I was worn out because Katherine kept waking up with panic attacks at 3 AM and when I told this to John he turned gray. He said he had been waking up at the same time with a feeling of great uneasiness (not panic attacks per se) since they stopped using the board. He chalked it up to a change in his work shift. He was taking some kind of vitamin supplement to regulate his sleep, so I got the name of it and bought some for Katherine in hopes that it would help her (and me) sleep.

A week or so after this meeting, I returned to Wausau to see a concert and brought Katherine with me. By this time it was winter, and we had time to kill before the show started, so I took Katherine for a walk downtown. It was Sunday and most of the businesses were closed, so after hanging out at the bookshop and record shop we had run out of distractions. I suggested a walk across the railroad bridge to a little island in the middle of the Wisconsin River, locally known as "Body Island."

The island is down-river from Big Bull Falls, and one explanation for the name comes from this being the place where bodies in the Wisconsin wash up. In the nineteenth century, many lumberjacks drowned while dislodging logjams, and their remains ended up here. Some say the name comes from a woman that worked at Prange Way in the 1970s. [Prange Way was a department store; today the building is the Eastbay Corporate Offices.] She used to cross the trestle bridge as a short cut on her way home until one night when she vanished. After an all-night search, she was found on the tip of the island, staring into the water. She had been stabbed and was in shock and died at the hospital; what made this murder so memorable, though, was that her sister was killed a few years later in the cemetery where this woman was buried. Despite the morbid associations, Body Island is a pretty little preserve of wild grassland and offers a nice view of the city. [Its real name is Barker Stewart Island and it is named after the lumber company that once had a mill there. A few years ago a woman was beaten to death on the shore opposite the island.]

Katherine and I were walking along the track when something got my attention. I don't remember what it was, but I climbed down from the bridge to the riverbank to look, while Katherine waited on the wind-swept trestle. While she was standing there, she heard a faint noise. At first she feared it was a train whistle—it is an active train bridge—but soon realized that the whistle sounded more human than locomotive. She felt the familiar sense of fear rising up inside, and when I returned she was having a full-blown panic attack. She said she heard something, but as much as I tried I couldn't. Then she heard it again, as "if it was right over my shoulder." Still, I heard nothing, and after we left the bridge Katherine suffered from panic attacks for the rest of the day.

Back in Sun Prairie, we found a message from John on the answering machine. He sounded upset, and when I met with him, he told me a strange story.

He had come home from work, and when he arrived at his room in the boarding house, had tried to do some drawings (John's hobby is art). He couldn't concentrate, though, and had an "uncanny feeling," so he decided to call us, not knowing that Katherine and I were out of town. Not finding any of his friends at home, he tried reading but couldn't. By this time it was late enough for him to get some sleep, but for some reason he couldn't stand lying in bed and decided to sleep on the floor. He fell fast asleep and at some point a knock on the door woke him up.

John's former boarding house in Madison, Wisconsin. The attic window to the left was his room.

"John," he heard Katherine say, "let's go out to breakfast!" We often stopped by to pick up John for breakfast on our way into Madison. It was a common enough thing. He got up and was looking for his clothes when he noticed that it was still pitch black outside. He heard the voice again saying, "John. Let's go out for breakfast." It couldn't be us, not that early in the morning, and he was overcome by a fear so intense that he felt limp and lay back down on the floor. This time the voice, still sounding like Katherine, said, "John . . . open the door!" But he just lay on the floor where he could see hall light through the crack under the door and the shadow of someone standing outside. It went away but he did not sleep the rest of the night.

I told him that it couldn't have been us because we were in Wausau. He checked with the old woman and the man who lived across the hall to see if they had knocked on his door, but they all said no. The woman kept the front door locked at night, and she was the one who opened it for visitors. No one stopped by that night.

John still wonders what would've happened if he had opened that door.

Eye on the Bye-Bye Man

That was Eli's story.

Like most experiences of this kind, it does not have a satisfying resolution. Strange things happened, then they stopped happening, and that's about it. Of all the strange, allegedly true, stories I've been told, though, this is one of the few that ever spooked me.

Some of this may have been atmosphere. I heard it late one Halloween night in a small, overheated apartment lit by jack-o-lanterns and decorated with cardboard skeletons. The room was crowded with guests, so dozens of witches and ghosts were sitting lined up along the sofa or standing in corners, silently smoking cigarettes and absorbing the story of the Bye-Bye Man. I expect that reading it on a cool flat page has less impact than a first person account heard at midnight through an eye-watering fog of tobacco, hot cider, and burning pumpkin insides, but as soon as Eli had finished, my curiosity began kicking in. What really happened? Can any of it be proven? Did the Bye-Bye Man, or someone like him, ever exist?

Eli will admit to sacrificing accuracy for effect when telling the story at Halloween (e.g., describing the Ouija board as cursed or saying that the mysterious visitor knocked at 3 AM. John didn't actually notice the time, just that it was dark outside). When he finally wrote it all down, Eli was recalling events that took place thirteen years earlier. Distortions and memory lapses were inevitable, he had freely retold it numerous times, and nothing could be corroborated. The notebooks were lost long ago; John is difficult to find, as his job keeps him on the road, and Katherine refuses to discuss what happened.

One of the goals of their experiment had been finding a piece of verifiable information that could not have been known to the sitters. They did not do this but I have made an attempt. There is, however, almost nothing definite for a researcher to pursue except the orphanage and (possibly) the murders.

Algiers

Algiers is a real place. It is a part of New Orleans, and though it is detached from the rest of the city and lies on the west bank of the Mississippi, a bend in the river actually puts it east of the French Quarter.

New Orleans would make an appropriate backdrop to the Bye-Bye Man's story. Death can't be concealed in a city where the water table is so high that bodies are interred in sprawling above-ground mausoleums, and funeral processions are accompanied by Dixieland jazz-bands. It is haunted by the ghosts of a murdered Turkish sultan, slaves, and sadistic masters and is the historical center of voodoo (or, more properly, Voduon) in North America, with two museums devoted to the subject. Offerings are still left at the reputed tombs of Marie Laveau, Voodoo Queen of New Orleans, and Xs are penciled onto them for good luck. The city is most famous for the annual grotesqueries of Mardi Gras, but there is an atmosphere of romantic decay about it that has inspired artists as diverse as Walt Disney and resident author Anne Rice. Disneyland's Haunted Mansion can be found off New Orleans Square, while Rice's Lestat novels have made the city synonymous with decadent vampirism. But it's not all Spanish moss, gumbo, and vaporish belles languidly fanning themselves on the veranda. New Orleans is a port and rail city, and Algiers played a role in its development.

What started out as a village dominated by enormous sugar plantations gave way to dry docks, ironworks, and warehouses when the riverfront was turned into a center for the ship repair business. In 1870, Algiers was incorporated into the city. Author Bill Sasser describes it today as "a part of New Orleans that most visitors never see. Its small Baptist churches, dangerous looking bars, dilapidated houses, and vacant industrial lots are home to some of America's worst urban poverty and crime, but good people also live honest lives there, in a culture steeped in spirituality and religion."[28]

Vodoun is a part of that spirituality and Algiers has long been identified with magic; it is even mentioned in songs like J. B. Lenoir's "Voodoo Boogie."

I flew to Algiers, I sure had a wonderful time
I flew to Algiers, and I sure had a wonderful time
I met a voodoo woman who was changin' a poor man's mind[29]

The one fact in the Spirit of the Board's story that seemed most likely to produce results was the orphanage. I contacted the Algiers Historical Society and was told that there had not been one there but there had been one in Gretna, "a couple of miles up river."[30] The author of a history of Gretna, however, told me that she was not aware of any orphanages there either. What if it were a different kind of institution? There is a danger of casting too wide a net, but the Bye-Bye Man's albinism, deteriorating eyesight, and erratic behavior suggested he might have been in a home for disabled children. One such home turned out to be on the border between Algiers and Plaquemines Parish, the Belle Chasse State School. This looked promising but it was founded in 1967[31] and could not have played a part in the story. (On the plus side, the school is less than a thousand feet from train tracks and the road where it's located is said to be haunted by a creature with glowing eyes and a were-wolf known as the "Rue-Ga-Rue."[32])

My search for the orphanage or a reasonable equivalent has *not* been exhaustive (there are still several avenues that need investigating), but what about the crimes? Assuming the story is true, do any known murders correspond to those carried out by the Bye-Bye Man? It's possible.

The Southern Pacific's Texas & New Orleans Railroad yard is in Algiers, and when the Bye-Bye Man fled the city it may have been on one of their trains. According to the Spirit of the Board, the murders began in the late 1920s or early 1930s, and it was around this time that mangled bodies began showing up thirteen hundred miles to the north.

The Mad Butcher
Between 1934 and 1939, an unknown killer known as "The Cleveland Torso Killer" or the "Mad Butcher of Kingsbury Run"

murdered at least sixteen men and women. The victims were fringe dwellers, transients, and prostitutes, who were killed by decapitation and their neatly dismembered remains left around Kingsbury Run. This is a gully running through downtown Cleveland, Ohio, that is "lined with 30-odd pairs of railroad tracks serving local factories and distant cities, bearing cargo to Pittsburgh, Chicago or Youngstown . . . During the Great Depression . . . [it] was also a favorite campsite for hoboes . . ."[33] Similar murders appeared in cities with rail links to Cleveland, with headless bodies found in boxcars from Youngstown, Ohio, and near the tracks in New Castle and West Pittsburgh, Pennsylvania.

The chief investigator of the "torso" case, Det. Peter Merylo, believed that the same killer was responsible for between forty and fifty murders. Despite many bizarre theories (including a mad scientist "attempting to graft human eyes and ears onto the tin skull of a mechanical robot"[34]), investigators believed "the Butcher rode the rails, picked his victims from among the ranks of the hobo populations with which he traveled, and carried out his murder-dismemberments in railroad cars."[35]

The disappearance of a hobo may go unnoticed and unreported outside of hobo circles. In 1997, Salem, Oregon, Police Detective Mike Quackenbush told *The Spokesman-Review*: "You can kill a transient and (the body) may not surface for two weeks . . . The suspect, by that time, may be 20 states away."[36] And when bodies are found, someone else may get the blame. A loosely knit organization of hoboes called the Freight Train Riders of America, for example, has been accused of committing three hundred murders a year! Headless bodies are also less likely to be identified, and several victims of the Butcher remain John and Jane Does.

Despite years of police work and a procession of odd suspects, including a "voodoo doctor" and a man who had an uncommon physical response to seeing chickens slaughtered, the killer was never found. Was it the Bye-Bye Man?

Decapitation would be in line with his interest in eyes and tongues, the head could be carried away and parts removed at leisure, but of the sixteen accepted "torso" slayings, the heads of eight were recovered. Some of these were skulls, but none of the fresher remains showed signs of mutilation beyond a severed neck. This suggests it was not the Bye-Bye Man. (A pair of scissors is the only weapon mentioned in connection with him, and they were used in a stabbing.) Finally, the first bodies appeared in Pennsylvania in 1925, a few years earlier than Eli's story would suggest. More research may turn up murders committed at the right time and accompanied by the Bye-Bye Man's signature mutilations, but until then, there is no evidence to show that he's killed anyone.

Without an orphanage or evidence of murders, the story appears to be an invention. But who invented it and why? Perhaps the answers can be found in two of the popular interpretations of Ouija board phenomena discussed earlier: spirits and the sitters' subconscious.

Spirits are credited with a wide range of moral and intellectual qualities, and their motives for creating a story like the Bye-Bye Man would reflect that; it could have been a simple prank by mischievous spirits, or something more sinister, like a case of attempted possession.

Unclean Spirits

Possession is usually defined as control of a living being by an external disembodied agent. It might be a spirit, a god, or the soul of someone who has died. There are, of course, numerous exceptions. (Corpses and animals can be taken over by spirits, and many cultures recognize possession by living, supernatural beings with bodies like the *jinn* of the Middle East.) The popular image of an adolescent girl floating over a mattress spewing profanities and pea soup is just one manifestation of a widespread and complex phenomenon, the main function of which is religious. Possession allows spirits to speak and act directly in this world; it remains an essential practice in "the shamanism of the North American Indians and the aborigines of Siberia, in the devotional states of the early European saints and in the possession dances of African and New World Negro."[37] Today, there are many Pentecostal and charismatic forms of Christian worship that actively seek possession by the Holy Spirit.

If we proceed on the assumption that spirits were involved in Wisconsin, taking part in the séances and the manifestations that followed, there is nothing to suggest they were benign. The manipulation of the sitters, the Bye-Bye Man's gruesome story, sleep disturbances, frightening paranormal phenomena, and an overall climate of fear all point to the efforts of "evil spirits."

"Evil spirits" is an elastic term that can be applied to anything from goblins to vampires. Here it refers to the souls of wicked people who have died, or hate-filled, malevolent intelligences that have never lived: demons, devils, and/or fallen angels. Either kind of evil spirit can cause possession but the "symptoms" may differ.

When souls of the dead are responsible, the victim may exhibit traits belonging to the deceased: their mannerisms, special knowledge, likes or dislikes, even allergic reactions. Demoniacs, the demonically possessed, display preternatural knowledge of the past, present, and future; speak and understand foreign and ancient languages unknown to the victim; are repelled by religion and everything associated with it; and are associated with some paranormal phenomena. Also, like angels dancing on the head of a pin, any number of evil spirits can possess a victim at the same time.

Jesus expelled a multitude of demons called "Legion" from the Gadarene demoniac into a herd of swine, which charged into the sea and drowned. A more recent case (not involving livestock) was an exorcism performed by Father Theophilus Riesinger on an adult woman in Earling, Iowa, in 1928. The priest successfully drove out spirits claiming to be the demon Beelzebub, along with the souls of the victim's father, the father's mistress, and even Judas Iscariot.[38] In life, the victim's father had been an exceptionally evil character, who cursed her for not taking part in his depravities. The curse is believed to have resulted in her demonic possession, but this is uncommon.

Medieval and Renaissance authorities believed possession could result from witchcraft or illness, but the likeliest cause was the victim's own sinfulness. They might be guilty of serious transgressions, as when "in 531 Theodoric's army had entered the capital of

Auvergne . . . pillaged the basilica and committed several acts of abomination, which caused them . . . to be possessed by the devil."[39] But the sins could also be comparatively light. The *Malleus Maleficarum* tells the story of "a hermit of upright and pious life" named Moses, who "engaged in a dispute with the Abbot Macharius, and [when he] went a little too far in the expression of a certain opinion, he was immediately delivered up to a terrible devil, who caused him to void his natural excrements through his mouth."[40] A single thoughtless act might have disastrous consequences. There was a nun in fifth-century Italy, for instance, who failed to make the sign of the Cross before eating a lettuce leaf, swallowed a demon that happened to be sitting on it, and had to be exorcized.

This view of possession as a casual event, and demons as something akin to germs, is now uncommon in the west. The controversial, but widely read, author, exorcist, and former Jesuit priest Malachi Martin (1921–1999) believed that evil spirits concentrate on perverting the will, not the body, and they must have cooperation. "At every new step," he wrote, "and during every moment of possession, the consent of the victim is necessary, or possession cannot be successful."[41] This consent can be subtle, almost unconscious, or as straightforward as a signed contract between the possessed and the devil, but it must be there. (Though, the Roman Catholic Church does recognize rare instances when "God seems sometimes to allow even the innocent to be exposed to the physical violence of the Devil."[42]) Martin describes possession as a four-step process.

- The entry point "at which Evil Spirit enters an individual and a decision, however tenuous, is made by the victim to allow that entry."
- Erroneous judgments "by the possessed in vital matters, as a direct result of the allowed presence of the possessing spirit and apparently in preparation for the next stage."
- Voluntary yielding of control "by the possessed person to a force or presence he clearly feels is alien to himself and as a result of which the possessed loses control of his will, and so of his decisions and his actions."

- Perfect possession. This is not the swearing, floating,
  and paranormal phenomena kind of possession,
  but a functioning, apparently normal condition
  that leaves the person devoid of humanity.[43]

It would require detailed biographies of each sitter to find evidence
of the process at work, along with greater powers of discernment
than mine, but aspects of their lives do suggest a vulnerability or
openness to diabolical forces.

The Sitters

Eli and John both enjoy horror as entertainment, but their
interest goes beyond movies, novels, and role-playing games. Both
are writers, and Eli is especially prolific, producing books, stories,
and plays with macabre themes. He has a degree in folklore, is
well read on the subject of serial murder, took part in the Goth
sub-culture, which is fascinated with death, and spent many years
involved in parapsychology. This included working as the librarian
at the American Society for Psychical Research and carrying out
funded research into psychometry and numerous field investigations
of strange phenomena.

John studies philosophy, mysticism, and the work of Joseph
Campbell. He has a special interest in what might be called "fear
theory," the how and why of what makes things frightening, and
a history of paranormal experiences. Growing up in a "haunted-
looking" house outside Stevens Point, John once saw the face of an
old woman appear in the bathroom mirror. She told him, "I am your
mother!" But it was not his mother.

Katherine takes no pleasure in horror. At the time of the séances
she was a radical feminist hipster "Riot Grrrl" with tattoos and
piercings who was studying feminist spirituality and had some
unusual experiences of her own. One of these took place when she
and a friend made an impromptu trip to a cabin in the countryside.
No one knew they were there, but soon after they arrived, the phone
rang. Her friend picked up and a voice that sounded like a little
girl asked to speak to Katherine. Being in a cabin in the woods and

getting a phone call from an unknown child was very weird, so they hung up. The phone began ringing again and they left.

Despite being born and raised in Wisconsin, where there are "more ghosts per square mile than any state in the nation,"[44] Eli has never seen or had a paranormal experience. He has spent long hours in graveyards, haunted houses, and Satanic churches; worked with psychics, Wiccans, and sorcerers; and in spite of all these efforts, remains supernaturally *virgo intacta*.

All three participants held unconventional social, spiritual, and political opinions, enjoyed offbeat subjects, and were leading lives that traditional moralists would describe as sinful. By itself, this should not be especially attractive to demons; if it were, college campuses across the U.S. would be overrun by evil spirits (and doubtless some people believe they are). It may have been the introduction of an occult element in the form of the Ouija board, however, that transformed the situation.

Hell Bait?

Consider events from the perspective of demonic activity. Three relatively normal young people hold a series of séances. They contact spirits that have never lived and receive long dull messages. Interest wanes. At this point, the spirits drop hints about dark dangerous things too frightening to discuss. This appeals to John and Eli, but not Katherine, who must be persuaded to continue. The sitters "force" the spirits to cooperate and, with a show of great reluctance, the Spirit of the Board tells them the history of the Bye-Bye Man. This story is gruesome by itself, but in combination with the formula, "if you think about him, he will find you," it is turned into a kind of mental invocation for summoning evil forces to the thinker.

The séances ended before establishing contact with the Bye-Bye Man but by then, to use a military analogy, the invaders had already established a bridgehead in the sitters' territory. They proceeded to soften up resistance by disturbing the sleep of John and Katherine (who woke Eli). While the spirits' aims are unknown, John's experience with the mysterious caller suggests an attempt at possession—it may, in fact, have been one of the stages described by Malachi Martin. If so, it was carried out when the target was at his most vulnerable: asleep, alone, and in what might have been a disturbed emotional state (we will return to the subject of John's frame of mind). The knocking and request that he "open the door" can be interpreted metaphorically or perhaps the physical act itself would have constituted assent.

In Katherine's case, the paranormal inspires such terror that she seems to be a poor candidate for possession. Perhaps the demons saw in her tendency to panic, an opportunity for another kind of deviltry, and the whistling on the bridge was an attempt to frighten Katherine into jumping off or falling into the Wisconsin River. It's safe to assume that demons have the worst possible motives for whatever they do.

John's and Katherine's experiences recall an old description of the Devil as a kind of tapeworm, a "slender incomprehensible spirit" that can "easily insinuate and wind himself into human bodies, and, cunningly couched in our bowels, vitiate our healths, terrify our souls with fearful dreams and shake our minds with furies."[45] From the sitters' backgrounds to the manifestations themselves, almost every aspect of the story can be interpreted in terms of evil spirits, but this requires accepting the existence of beings for which no evidence exists. Demons are hypothetical but the sitters are real; what if the people involved are the source of everything that happened, including the Spirit of the Board's story and seemingly paranormal phenomena?

Pieces of the Bye-Bye Man

While the ultimate source of the Bye-Bye Man will probably remain unknown, we can approach the story like a scientist studying an unfamiliar animal. Different aspects of its anatomy can reveal what it does, where it came from, and what it might be related to. A closer look at parts of the Bye-Bye Man's history could, in the same way, tell us something about its origins, deeper meanings, or historical reality.

His Name

The Bye-Bye Man's name recalls the fiends that are said to haunt lovers' lanes, summer camps, and dark stretches of woods. Folklorist Jan Brunvand's collective term for these monsters and lunatics is "teenage horrors," the most famous representative of which is "the Hook" or "Hookman." There are many others, including a "Green Man," "Goat Man," "Squirrelman," and "Bunny Man." (The Hook was an escaped homicidal maniac who, for some reason, had been fitted with a sharp steel prosthetic hook. Accidental electrocution turned the Green Man green, and now he only goes out at night to peek into car windows. The back roads of Prince George's County, Maryland, are frequented by an axe-swinging goat-centaur or goat-headed sasquatch called the Goat Man; the rest have similar descriptions.)

Unlike these examples, the meaning of the name "Bye-Bye Man" remains obscure. It could be a garbled version of a real name (B. B. Mann, Bobby Mann, Bubba Mann), a reference to how dangerous he is ("say good-bye"), or the kind of nickname used by hoboes and criminals. In Jack Black's 1926 autobiography, *You Can't Win*, the author describes a world of train-hopping safecrackers, winos, and thieves who knew each other as "Gold Tooth," "Smiler," and the "Sanctimonious Kid." While the meaning of "Bye-Bye Man" remains a riddle, it is the single most important part of the story.

Folklore contains many examples of secret names and their power. Rumpelstiltskin lost his claim to the princess's baby when she learned his name, and Jewish folklore tells of miracle workers like Rabbi Judah Loew ben Bezalel of Prague who used the secret name of God to turn a pile of clay into a living golem. Children can summon a witch called Mary Worth by looking into a mirror and repeating her name three times (which recalls John's odd experience with a mirror).

To know the Bye-Bye Man's name and think about it, however, is to steal away some important part of him, something that he is compelled to retrieve through murder and mutilation.

Albinism

One of the most striking features of the Bye-Bye Man himself is whiteness. He suffers from albinism, a "Congenital absence of pigment from the skin, hair, choroid coat, and iris,"[46] that many societies regard with suspicion. White is often considered a symbol of purity and virginity, but in Chapter 42 of *Moby Dick* Herman Melville discusses how an absence of color intensifies what is frightening. He mentions white sharks, polar bears, and other examples before asking: "What is it that in the Albino man so peculiarly repels and often shocks the eye, as that sometimes he is loathed by his own kith and kin! It is that whiteness which invests him, a thing expressed by the name he bears. The Albino is as well made as other men—has no substantive deformity—and yet this mere aspect of all-pervading whiteness makes him more strangely hideous than the ugliest abortion."[47]

The Spirit of the Board did not mention the Bye-Bye Man's race, but Louisiana has many citizens of African descent, and if albinism is difficult for whites, it presents even greater problems for blacks.

Racism was an integral part of turn-of-the-century American society, but when fair skin confers superior rank, a black person who is whiter than a white person is disorienting for everyone. Besides raising uncomfortable questions about linking status to pigmentation, the albino was not white, black, or mixed and was likely to be rejected by all three. In an article presented by the National Organization for Albinism and Hypopigmentation (NOAH) entitled "African Americans with Albinism,"[48] the attitudes and responses the condition inspires in black communities are explored: "A basic theme in many variations in [sic] that God is delivering judgment on a family with albinism and that the individual with albinism is cursed, or is the embodiment of sin . . . Another belief is that the person with albinism is the result of incest or inbreeding. The most common myth of today is that the non-Caucasian person with albinism must be the result of mixed marriage."

If the Bye-Bye Man's mother was suspected of incest or adultery, it could have broken up the family, or led to his being put in an orphanage. It may even link his story with a series of unsolved murders that were committed "at stops along the Southern Pacific Rail Railroad line." Michael Newton writes in *Still at Large* that "Between January 1911 and April 1912, an unidentified killer (or killers) slaughtered 49 victims in the states of Louisiana and Texas, leaving police baffled. In each case, the dead were mulattos or black members of families with mulatto children. The killers were presumed, by blacks and law enforcement alike, to be dark-skinned Negroes, selecting victims on the basis of their mixed—or 'tainted'—blood."[49] The killer(s) could have also been of mixed race, driven to murder by self-loathing. Voduon was considered another possible motive.

Since the Bye-Bye Man's mother had a child with albinism, she may have been among the victims of the 1911–1912 murders. That would explain how he became an orphan, and if the Bye-Bye Man were born in those years, he would have been seventeen to eighteen years old in 1929, when the Great Depression began. On the other hand, the 1911 killings were not local; they began in the towns of Rayne, Lafayette, and Crowley, more than 150 miles west of Algiers.

The Bye-Bye Man was probably regarded as cursed from birth. Like the Wandering Jew and Cain, he seems to be a perpetual traveler with special powers, an extended lifespan, and something like two of the three marks of Cain. According to rabbinical literature, Cain had a horn on his head, a Hebrew letter branded on his arm, and "leprosy" in the form of spots on his skin, "which were brightly white and which sparkled like snow."[50] The Bye-Bye Man did not have a horn but there was an unidentified tattoo on his arm, and his skin was unnaturally pale. He is also a permanent inhabitant of the gray area between races and places where the paranormal flourishes.

Blindness

Albinism can affect vision, too. The eyes look pink and the person may have astigmatism and photophobia (intolerance or fear of light), but in the Bye-Bye Man's case, his eyesight deteriorated into blindness.

This can be interpreted symbolically as a separation from light, truth, and goodness, or as a manifestation of inner psychic light. The legendary Greek prophets Phineus and Tiresias, for example, were struck blind by the gods but also given the power of prophecy. On a more practical level, the Bye-Bye Man may wear glasses covered with paint along with a broad-brimmed hat because they provide some protection from the light. Other parts of his outfit, including the jacket that looks like a pea-coat, and the sack, possibly a duffel bag, suggest a nautical appearance that recalls his port city origins. The Bye-Bye Man's dark glasses, in association with the murders, magic, and New Orleans, also suggest a possible connection to the Guede, Vodoun spirits of the dead, who wear dark glasses but have little else in common. (The Guede and their chief, Baron Samedi, are earthy, sensual spirits preoccupied with eating, drinking, smoking, and sex.)

Blind monsters have never been common. The best known is probably Polyphemus, the Cyclops in Homer's *Odyssey*, whose single eye was put out by Odysseus, but they also appear in some horror movies. The Frankenstein monster loses his sight after receiving Ygor's brain in *Ghost of Frankenstein* (1942), and blind zombies appear in *Return of the Living Dead* (1985) and *Tombs of the Blind Dead* (1971).

The creatures in these last two films found their victims through the senses of smell or hearing; the Bye-Bye Man's ability to track down people thinking a specific thought seems to be unique. It has its limitations, though, or he would not need Gloomsinger.

Giving Tongue

We are given very few details about what Gloomsinger is or does. Presumably it acts like the Bye-Bye Man's hunting dog, using its eyes to find the prey and then signaling the position to his master by whistling.

The name is mysterious (perhaps a variation of "blues singer," which might be a link to New Orleans), and its appearance just as vague. Gloomsinger could be a humanoid thing or a shapeless mass that moves along on tongues like a train of little legs.

Popular culture may have also played a part here. Like the Frankenstein monster, Gloomsinger is made from pieces of different corpses, sutured together, and reanimated into a new being. The combination of eyes and tongues, however, has less in common with the philosophical novel of Mary Shelley than with the horror fiction of H. P. Lovecraft. Lovecraft (1890–1937) created a unique "mythos" of vast inter-dimensional entities called the "Old Ones," descriptions of which suggest the second version of Gloomsinger as seen through the wrong end of a telescope. Consider this passage from "The Dunwich Horror" (1929), in which a character, complete with rural New England accent, tries describing one:[51]

"Bigger'n a barn . . . all made o' squirmin' ropes . . . hull thing sort o' shaped like a hen's egg bigger'n anything, with dozens o' legs like hogsheads that haff shut up when they step . . . nothin' solid about it—all like jelly, an' made o' seprit wrigglin' ropes pushed clost together . . . great bulgin' eyes all over it . . . ten or twenty maouths or trunks a-stickin' aout all along the sides, big as stovepipes, an' all a-tossin' an' openin' an' shuttin' . . . all grey, with kinder blue or purple rings . . . *an' Gawd in heaven—that haff face on top! . . .*"

John, incidentally, is a Lovecraft fan, and a publisher specializing in the author's work, Arkham House, is in Sauk City, not far from Sun Prairie.

And what is Gloomsinger's nature? Is it demonic, like the imps that served as witch's familiars in the shapes of cats and toads, or something else? We are told that thinking of the name "Gloomsinger" is equally effective for summoning the Bye-Bye Man, which suggests that instead of being an independent being, it is an extension of its master, a detached "limb" able to move under its own power, but perishable and requiring regular maintenance.

Whatever its origins, Gloomsinger plays an unclear but essential role in the stalking, murdering, and mutilation attributed to the Bye-Bye Man. The most important question remains, of course, why did he do it at all?

Motivation

If the Voduon thread is followed back to Africa, we find mutilation murders reminiscent of the Bye-Bye Man's alleged crimes. A number of people are killed every year so that their limbs, tongues, eyes, and sex organs can be used for magical ingredients. These "muti" killings, however, occur in the southern part of the continent, and Voduon has its origins among the Yoruba people of West Africa. The ritual murders seen there involve different kinds of mutilations, with an emphasis on blood.[52] The Bye-Bye Man seems to have no use for body parts, beyond what's needed for keeping Gloomsinger in a state of repair, which suggests that he is not interested in the "trophies" or "souvenirs" collected by conventional serial killers.

Ordinary homicidal maniacs favor photographs of their victims, articles of clothing, and sometimes pieces of anatomy, but rarely eyes and tongues. (An exception was Charles Albright of Texas, who murdered three women in 1990–1991 and carefully removed their eyes.) There is also an enduring belief in the eyes' ability to retain an image of the last thing that a person sees, which has caused some killers to mutilate their victim's body. This may be, for example, why the Soviet-era murderer Andrei Chikatilo stabbed eyes. Among his other atrocities, Chikatilo also bit out tongues but does not seem to have collected them. None of this, however, explains why the Bye-Bye Man supposedly kills people who think of his name.

If the story is a product of the sitters' subconscious, then it may be comparable to a dream, which leaves it open to other kinds of interpretations.

Removing or destroying eyes often symbolizes castration. Eyes in combination with the tongue may represent the full complement of male reproductive organs and several elements in the story can be interpreted in terms of emasculation. There is the use of desk scissors as a weapon, the bloody "seaman's sack," and the female voice presumably used by the Bye-Bye Man, suggesting that he is a eunuch.

If the Bye-Bye Man's secret name is the essence of his power, then when someone learns that name, it may be equivalent to castration. Following this line of reasoning, the Bye-Bye Man's blindness represents the loss of his masculinity, and Gloomsinger—made from eyes and tongues—acts as substitute genitals. They are artificial, though, and subject to decay, requiring regular restoration, which may reflect a degree of male insecurity. When the Bye-Bye Man locates someone who is thinking of his name, he kills them and incorporates the organs into Gloomsinger, thereby recovering his power/masculinity. He is, at least temporarily, whole. The idea of male genitals being separated from the body and acting independently is found in several North American Trickster tales and recalls the ameboid sperm produced by some invertebrates. (Instead of being propelled by whip-like flagella, they crawl along on pseudopods in search of the egg.)

Was the Spirit of the Board's story an expression of sexual anxieties felt by the young men? Prader-Willi syndrome prevents the onset of sexual maturity; perhaps the residents inspired some insecurity? Could the source have been resentment felt by a woman pressured into continuing with a project that frightened her? It's possible, but it's also possible that this theory is a combination of my own apprehensions and a desire to find a rationale for the Bye-Bye Man's otherwise inexplicable behavior. Having taken that grain of salt we can now . . .

Return to Algiers

Algiers is the one indisputable fact in the whole story. If it sprang from the sitters' subconscious, where did they learn about a relatively obscure district of New Orleans? The most likely source is the 1987 film *Angel Heart*.

Angel Heart was adapted from the William Hjortsberg novel *Falling Angel* (1978). It tells the story of private detective Harold Angel, who has been hired by a wealthy and mysterious client named Louis Cyphre to find a singer suffering from amnesia. (For readers who collect coincidences, Harold Angel came from "A little place in Wisconsin you've never heard of. Just outside Madison."[53]) Almost all of the novel's action takes place in New York City, but the movie has

Angel travel down to New Orleans, where he becomes involved with voodoo, black magic, and murder. Film critic Roger Ebert wrote: "His odyssey in *Angel Heart* takes him from New York to Algiers, La., a town across from New Orleans that makes the fleshpots of Bourbon Street look like Disneyland."[54] The Algiers scenes were actually filmed in an abandoned plantation village called Laurel Valley Village in Thibodaux, Louisiana, which gives the impression that Algiers is a rural town.[55] This might explain why neither the sitters, the Spirit of the Board, nor Roger Ebert, seemed to know that it is a part of New Orleans. I watched *Angel Heart* before writing this and could not find any reference to it as a part of the city.

These are just some of the sources that may have contributed to the Bye-Bye Man's story; it contains nothing that requires paranormal involvement. Telepathy or other phenomena may have played a part—Eli saw suggestions of it during the séances—but psychic powers are not needed to explain where the story might have come from. This was not a laboratory experiment, so sitters talked about the messages they were getting, speculated freely, and may have been engaged in a "process of joint imaginative creation" that was expressed through the board.[56] With regard to Katherine's and John's experiences, however, the way the story was created may be less important than the effect it had once it existed. Did it frighten them into believing an attack of tinnitus and a vivid dream were supernatural? Or could the story itself have led to paranormal manifestations?

In the discussion of demons, it was suggested that the combination of the Bye-Bye Man story and the "if you think about him . . ." formula might have acted as a kind of mental invocation. What if the same method produced results without the intervention of invisible entities? We've discussed two explanations for the sitters' experiences so far, one based on spirits and the other on the human mind. What if "spirits" in the sense of paranormal manifestations were not a separate phenomenon, but one that originated with the participants themselves?

What if it was a manifestation of the "Philip Effect"?

The Imaginary Ghost

In 1972, the Society for Psychical Research in Toronto conducted an experiment that attempted to answer three questions: could séance phenomena be created in full light, are these phenomena produced by living people or disembodied spirits, and is a medium necessary for phenomena to occur? None of the eight participants considered themselves especially psychic or showed evidence of being a medium,[57] and they tried to answer these questions by creating a ghost of their own, an imaginary historical figure named Philip. Members of the society gave him a tragic and romantic background, similar to the legends associated with traditional ghosts.

They decided that "Philip was an aristocratic Englishman living in the middle 1600s at the time of Oliver Cromwell. He had been a supporter of the king and was a Catholic. He was married to a beautiful but cold and frigid wife, Dorothea, the daughter of a neighboring nobleman. One day, when out riding the boundaries of his estates, Philip came across a gypsy encampment and saw there a beautiful dark-eyed, raven-haired gypsy girl, Margo, and fell instantly in love with her.

"He brought her back secretly to live in the gatehouse near the stables of Diddington Manor—his family home. For some time he kept his love nest secret, but eventually Dorothea, realizing he was keeping someone else there, found Margo, and accused her of witchcraft and of stealing her husband. Philip was too scared of losing his reputation and his possessions to protest at the trial of Margo, and she was convicted of witchcraft and burned at the stake. Philip subsequently was stricken with remorse that he had not tried to defend Margo and use [sic] to pace the battlements of Diddington in despair. Finally, one morning his body was found at the foot of the battlements where he had cast himself in a fit of agony and remorse."[58]

The story was a mixture of fact and fiction with errors deliberately included to emphasize Philip's fictitious nature. There is, for instance, no record of a young, noble couple named Philip and Dorothea ever living at Diddington Manor, which is a real place. Also, English witches were normally hanged, not burned at the stake.

The society met once a week to work on their ghost. They would discuss Philip, talk about his life, interests, and how he would act in different situations. One member drew a portrait of him as a handsome young man with a beard. Sitting in a circle, the group would meditate on the drawing, trying to create a vivid picture of Philip in their minds that might turn into a visible apparition. Nothing significant happened, however, until the fall of 1973, when the group changed their approach. British parapsychologists Kenneth Batcheldor and Colin Brookes-Smith had been studying séance phenomena and recommended creating an "atmosphere of jollity and relaxation," so the members began sitting around a table, singing silly songs, eating candy, telling jokes, and addressing the table directly as Philip.[59]

Rosemary Ellen Guiley described the results of their experiment in her *Encyclopedia of Mystical & Paranormal Experiences*: "After the Owen group [Dr. A. R. G. Owen, director of the project] conducted several sessions, the table began to vibrate, resound with raps and knocks, and move seemingly of its own accord. Philip then began to communicate by rapping in response to questions.

"Philip answered questions consistent with his fictitious history, but could produce nothing beyond what the group had conceived. Philip also gave historically accurate information concerning real events and people. The Owen group theorized this material came from their own collective unconscious.

"Sessions with Philip continued for several years. A levitation and movement of the table were recorded on film in 1974. Efforts to capture Philip's voice on tape were inconclusive. Members of the group thought whispers were made in response to questions . . ."[60]

They never succeeded in producing a visible apparition, and neither did other groups that used the same methods to create "ghosts" like "Lilith," a French-Canadian spy executed in France during World War II; "Axel," a man from the future; "Santa Claus," "Silk the Dolphin," and others.

If these results have been accurately reported, then people willing to accept propositions they know to be untrue can produce paranormal phenomena under certain conditions. This has profound implications for science, religion, and the occult, and makes an interesting comparison to the theories advanced by Fred Beck. (See "The Devil's Militia.") Could the situation in Wisconsin, though produced accidentally, have generated the Bye-Bye Man? There are similarities between the two groups but also important differences, and these may explain the varying results.

The Toronto society set out to answer definite questions, and their results reflect this deliberate approach, producing phenomena that were consistent, long-lasting, repeatable, and limited. Philip was also approached cautiously, with steps taken to "contain" the project.

"The group always met in one particular room which was designated as 'Philip's room,' and not used for any other purpose. It had been agreed that if any kind of manifestation of Philip's presence was obtained, he should be confined to one room. There was a specific reason for all this. Until it was known in what form his manifestation might occur, it was felt safer to ensure that this only occurred when the group was together."[61] The room also contained pictures of Diddington Manor and period objects like books, documents, pictures, and fencing foils. (Philip loved fencing.) Manifestations were eventually produced in other places, but only through a group effort; they never occurred spontaneously or to sitters who were by themselves.

The artificial ghosts were also placed outside the sitters' time. Philip, Lilith, and Axel were either dead or had not yet been born and, as "spirits," could not be expected to appear outside of the séance room. Furthermore, they were all benign characters, so if any phenomena did happen to "leak" out, they would probably reflect this. The sitters had placed at least four lines of defense between themselves and their creations: the ghosts were self-evidently imaginary, their fictional lives were over or had not yet begun, they had harmless personalities, and their ability to produce phenomena depended on the presence of the group.

As for those who took part, Dr. Owen said of them: "The

members of the group are regarded as perfectly normal people, or as normal as people can actually be."[62] Their willingness and ability to take part in a long-term project also points to stable personal lives and careers.

In Wisconsin, the situation was very different. The sitters were looking for evidence of telepathy or verifiable spirit communication through casual experiments with a Ouija board; it was an impromptu arrangement that produced unforeseen results.

Unlike Philip, the sitters had not deliberately created the Bye-Bye Man. There was no attempt to create a vivid mental picture or contact him directly or produce manifestations. In fact, the séances ended almost immediately after the story emerged. Why then did Katherine and John, despite comparatively small investments in time and emotion, describe phenomena that were more dramatic than those connected with Philip?

There aren't many rules that can be applied to strange phenomena, except perhaps that you run out of film right before something interesting happens. Certain elements and conditions, however, seem to be associated with the paranormal and when these are present, manifestations may be more dramatic, if short-lived and unreliable, than those seen in Toronto.

Spontaneity is one of them. Impressive phenomena rarely occur under controlled conditions, and while there are exceptions (remote-viewing claims to be one), it is normally the difference between a parapsychologist detecting blips of telekinesis with statistical analysis and a poltergeist flinging furniture through the air. The Bye-Bye Man, like the poltergeist, appeared spontaneously.

Emotion is another element. The most useful one for generating séance-type phenomena seems to be "jollity" when experienced by the sitters, but powerful emotions like passion, guilt, and desire are traditionally associated with ghosts and played an important part in Philip's fictional biography. What if, instead of "Philip" the romantic knight, the Toronto group had tried to create "Phil," a happily married grocer who liked crossword puzzles and died in his sleep? Would it have worked? In contrast with the powerful but artificial emotions used in Philip, the Bye-Bye Man was created against a backdrop of genuine fear, dislocation, and sexual tension.

Emotional Impact?

Fear is an important element in this account. John and Eli shared a fascination with it, while Katherine was subject to panic attacks. Did the possibility of actually confronting their creation face to face, in an uncontrolled situation, create an element of fear that was absent in the Philip experiment, and produce results that Philip could not?

The Bye-Bye Man, after all, was not consciously created and his existence could not be disproved. He claimed to be a living being, not a disembodied spirit, and was threatening to kill and mutilate the sitters. Even if the group believed the story came from their subconscious, there may be a corner of our brains, some convolution inherited from millions of years of bug-eating, tree-dwelling ancestors, that regards all threats as real.

Danger creates intense feelings and may have produced manifestations without the conscious effort required by Philip. When seemingly paranormal phenomena occurred, however, John's experience was more elaborate and frightening than Katherine's and that may have been due to other factors in his life.

John was in a state of transition. He had just dropped out of college, worked as a dishwasher, lived in boarding houses, and was not in a relationship; in almost every respect, he was adrift in "the gap between old and new."[63]

People making the change from old to new, especially those experiencing important milestones like birth, puberty, marriage, and death, are traditionally believed to be vulnerable to supernatural forces. Countless rituals have been devised to keep them safe while the change is occurring and to help complete the process. While John was not going through one of the recognized transitions, it was a stressful, ill-defined period that may have intensified his experience with the Bye-Bye Man. Katherine's comparatively stable life may, in contrast, have moderated hers.

The classic connection between a state of transition and

unexplained phenomena is the pubescent child, usually a girl, found at the center of so many poltergeist cases. There are many other examples, but the apparent relationship between transformation and the paranormal may even apply to physical space. "In-between" spots—places that exist to be passed through, like stairways, doorways, and windows—are frequently associated with strange phenomena. John's and Katherine's experiences, for instance, involved a bridge and hallway. The effect is even seen in buildings undergoing renovations, when places with no reputation for ghosts become the scene of spooky goings-on, while previously haunted spots see their ghosts vanish for good. Either way, it's usually blamed on "disturbing the spirits."

One more complicated (and complicating) emotion may have been a by-product of the séances themselves. When the board began producing messages, the trio fell into specific roles: Eli devised experiments and motivated the sitters, while Katherine acted as medium, but only in combination with John, whose part was essential but difficult to define. The pair seemed to be attuned to the paranormal and each other in a way that Eli was not. It suggests there was a rapport between them; there certainly was an attraction.

Using a Ouija board requires a great deal of time spent in intimate physical contact, with glances and pheromones being exchanged over the planchette, and it was not long after the events described here that Eli and Katherine separated and she began seeing John.

While there's nothing unusual about a break-up, the paranormal seems to stimulate irrational lust the way it does irrational fear. It may not be a coincidence that the Greek god of the wild and primitive, Pan, caused "pan-ic" and was depicted in a state of chronic physical excitement. According to a friend who investigates haunted houses, the people who ask for help frequently display inappropriate, and seemingly uncharacteristic, forwardness towards investigators. There's no way of knowing if this played a part in John and Katherine's mutual attraction, but sex and guilt were added to the already overheated atmosphere of the séance room.

In contrast to the complicated emotions and casual approach

seen in Wisconsin, the Toronto Society was cool and systematic. They developed techniques for creating a limited number of repeatable, verifiable phenomena, while keeping potentially disruptive elements under control and insulating the participants against unforeseen results. Several of these disruptive elements were present with the Bye-Bye Man and none of the safeguards, which may have resulted in phenomena that were dramatic, but also ephemeral and subjective. Eli stood next to Katherine on the railroad bridge and heard nothing, while John's experience might have been a dream.

But what if he was awake? And what if John's account of what happened that night is accurate?

Other Artificial Entities

The American Academy of Science recognizes parapsychology as a science, and Philip was a scientific experiment carried out by a group of researchers. But what if they had called themselves a coven, and described what they were doing as magic? It probably would have had similar results. Spiritualists, sorcerers, and parapsychologists may differ in their assumptions about what's being done and why, but they share a common goal—acquiring some degree of control over paranormal phenomena. Mystics of every description have been working on the problem for millennia.

Some have regarded occult powers as a side issue in the pursuit of higher spiritual development, while others were interested in the tangible benefits of wealth, influence, love, and revenge. Numerous theories were needed to make the magical/paranormal comprehensible and provide a framework within which the operator could achieve results. Among the concepts are two that may help us understand the Bye-Bye Man: the "thought-form" and the "artificial elemental."

Definitions vary, but a thought-form is essentially a "non-physical entity created by thought,"[64] while an artificial elemental is similar, but infused with strong emotion. Individuals and groups can create these beings deliberately or accidentally, but "The phenomena produced consciously, with a view of bringing about a prescribed result . . . are generally—but not always—the work of a single person."[65] Thought-forms normally exist on the mental or astral sphere where they are invisible to all but the psychic or unusually sensitive, though other less finely tuned individuals may sense their presence. The French scholar, traveler, and writer Madame Alexandra David-Neel describes a number of different kinds of thought-forms in her 1929 book, *Magic and Mystery in Tibet*.

The durable David-Neel (1868–1969) was a Buddhist who spent fourteen years in Tibet and surrounding countries studying mysticism with swamis, hermits, and lamas. She describes a number of magical phenomena including "messages carried on the wind" (telepathy), enchanting a knife so that a selected victim will use it to commit suicide, *tumo* (the ability to generate high temperatures in the body), and the creation of the thought-form or *tulpa*. David-Neel experimented with the latter. She spent months in solitary meditation, carried out certain rituals, and successfully created "a monk, short and fat, of an innocent and jolly type."[66]

At first, it required concentration for David-Neel to see her *tulpa*, but it soon appeared without effort, while remaining invisible to others. The mind-monk traveled with her party and obeyed commands, but over time it grew less cherubic and more independent: "The fat, chubby-cheeked fellow grew leaner, his face assumed a vaguely mocking, sly, malignant look. He became more troublesome and bold. In brief, he escaped my control."[67]

David-Neel believed this process was inevitable. "Once the *tulpa* is endowed with enough vitality to be playing the part of a real being, it tends to free itself from its maker's control. This, say Tibetan occultists, happens nearly mechanically, just as the child, when his body is completed and able to live apart, leaves its mother's womb."[68] She accepted the possibility that the monk was the result of auto-suggestion (i.e., it was all in her imagination), except "a herdsman who brought me a present of butter saw the *tulpa* in my tent and took it for a live lama."[69] (Was the herdsman clairvoyant? Was the figure materializing in this world? The author does not offer an opinion.)

Over time, the monk's presence became so disturbing that David-Neel was forced to dissolve it, a task that required "six months of hard struggle. My mind-creature was tenacious of life."[70]

A *tulpa* can also appear spontaneously. It might happen to a traveler "passing through some sinister tract of country,"[71] and Western mountain-climbers have reported experiences that could be related to *tulpa*-lore. When, for example, Reinhold Messner made a solo ascent of Mt. Everest in 1980 he "imagined that an invisible companion was climbing beside him."[72] (Alpinists see and hear many strange things, but they also suffer from fatigue and lack of oxygen.) In cases where the *tulpa* is created unconsciously, and "the author or authors . . . does not aim at a fixed result," the outcome may be something like the phenomena described by John and Katherine, with bits and pieces of the thought-form's persona realized in paranormal form.

Had the séances continued, these "scraps" of Bye-Bye Man might have coalesced into something more formidable and the results might have been fatal. David-Neel describes instances of magicians being killed by the thought-forms they created. Perhaps "the more you think about him, the more dangerous he becomes" aspect of the story was a warning, not an invocation. Another possibility is that the group, or members of it, created a similar being called an artificial elemental.

The British occultist Dion Fortune described her encounter with this phenomenon in *Psychic Self-Defense* (1930). Fortune had been betrayed by a friend and was lying in bed, sleepily contemplating revenge, when "I felt a curious drawing out sensation from my solar plexus, and there materialised beside me on the bed a large wolf. It was a well materialised ectoplasmic form . . . grey and colourless, and . . . had weight. I could distinctly feel its back pressing against me as it lay beside me on the bed as a large dog might."[73]

The apparition was distinctly evil, and unlike David-Neel's monk, did not obey commands. Its nature was fixed by the emotions that caused it to appear in the first place, and had Fortune not reabsorbed it, the "were-wolf" would have gone on to create more evil. The experience was exhausting, but Fortune believed it had taught her a method for creating artificial elementals.

1. The actor needs to be in "the condition between sleeping and waking . . ."
2. Their mood has to be one of "brooding highly charged with emotion . . ."
3. They have to make an "invocation of the appropriate natural force . . ."[74]

Did John, like Fortune, unknowingly carry out these steps? He had not been sleeping well and was spending the night on the floor; perhaps, he was half-awake. There's no way of knowing his mental state, but he was no longer seeing Eli and Katherine regularly and earlier that evening had been unable to reach any friends. John may have been bored, lonely, or even "brooding." It seems unlikely that anything so dramatic as invoking a natural force was involved (Fortune claims to have been thinking about the mythical wolf Fenris right before the figure materialized), but the séances had just ended and the Bye-Bye Man was a recent memory.

Did John experience frustration, desire, resentment, and guilt that night? Did this formless but potent mixture of thoughts and feelings cast into the shape of the Bye-Bye Man? If so, it was unlike Fortune's were-wolf in that it seems to have embodied not revenge, but emotional conflict.

Ambivalence seems to be at the heart of John's story. Picture the scene. It is the middle of the night and a young man is asleep. He hears a knock on the door and a voice calling to him. It is the woman he is attracted to and she's asking to be let into his bedroom. Does John bang into furniture and overturn lamps in his race to the door? No, he goes limp with fear and lies on the floor in a state of terror till morning. Whatever happened, whether this was a thought-form, artificial elemental, bad dream, or other phenomenon, Katherine seems to have excited strong emotions in John, but he was either unwilling or afraid to act on them. Perhaps the castration symbols in the Bye-Bye Man's story express guilt over contemplated sexual misconduct. Violating sexual taboos and patricide drove King Oedipus to put out his eyes.

It may be that the Wisconsin group's haphazard approach resulted in an undefined, loosely constructed being that tried to fulfill its creators' expectations by killing anyone thinking about Gloomsinger or the Bye-Bye Man. Its appearance outside John's room and attempt to enlist his cooperation, however, suggests that it operated under certain restrictions. Perhaps these were incorporated into its make-up from the ragbag of sources presumed to have gone into creating the story. Like the consent needed by demons, there is a tradition that evil spirits cannot cross the threshold without being invited. The invitation can be obtained through threats, coaxing, or deceptions (like imitating Katherine's voice), but without it they are powerless. "The concept . . . probably evolved out of the Christian tradition that the devil cannot go where he is not welcome."[75]

If the Wisconsin group did create a monster, what happened to it? With the end of the séances and the breaking up of the collective mind, did it fade away? Or is the Bye-Bye Man lying dormant but potentially dangerous, like a hibernating rattlesnake? Fortune wrote that the artificial elemental's existence is "akin to that of an electric battery, it slowly leaks out by means of radiation, and unless recharged periodically, will finally weaken and die out."[76] Does "die out" mean total extinction, or is the Bye-Bye Man (or the potential for it) floating aimlessly in whatever ether these things inhabit, waiting to be revived through the power of thought? Perhaps it will only be gone when it is entirely forgotten.

Dion Fortune and David-Neel, however, were playing by occult game rules. Our culture is generally dubious about "Fiends who materialize out of nothing and nowhere, like winged pigweed and Russian thistle."[77] This may be just as well, as David-Neel mentions another possibility that is not pleasant to contemplate. "Tibetan magicians . . . relate cases in which the *tulpa* is sent to fulfil a mission, but does not come back and pursues its peregrinations as a half-conscious, dangerously mischievous puppet."[78]

Fortunately, there is no evidence to suggest the Bye-Bye Man actually exists—nothing except an occasional, disturbing news story.

Odd Hat, Dark Suit

On November 6, 2001, in the small town of Florence, Montana, three grandmothers had their throats cut in the middle of the day in a beauty salon next to a five-lane highway and less than five hundred feet from railroad tracks. The killer has not been caught but witnesses were able to describe him.

"Ravalli County Sheriff Perry Johnson said the sketches were the result of several interviews with people in the area who got a good look at the man who wore an odd hat and was dressed either in a dark suit or a duster-type coat."

The *Headwater News of the Rockies* reported that "The man had no facial hair, and is in his 20s, around 6 feet tall, with a slender build.

"He was wearing a white shirt with no tie and could have been carrying something when he was seen south of town.

"Authorities also released a photo of a pair of black-rimmed sunglasses that they have determined did not belong to any of the women at the salon. It's not known if they were left there by another customer or the killer."[79]

The odd, neat face staring out from under the brim of the black hat on the wanted poster was not the Bye-Bye Man. If the suspect suffered from albinism, the witnesses could hardly have missed it, and there was no hint that he was blind. The victims did not have the signature mutilations, and no mention is made of the Sack of Gore or paint on the sunglasses. There's just the crime, an odd costume, the killer's unexplained getaway, and train tracks nearby.

Like our less cautious, bug-eating ancestors, we may have ventured too far out onto some very slender limbs here; let's restore perspective by closing this story where it began, in America's dairy-land.

A Walk Across the Bridge

Before writing this book I visited Wisconsin and saw some of the places and things mentioned in the story.

The Ouija board that led the sitters to "The Spirit of the Board" has not been used since the last séance and is kept locked inside a closet in a rural cabin. It is one of several vaguely supernatural objects owned by Eli, including a bar of soap from a haunted sink, a book of black magic, and a cursed monkey spear (the curse was aimed at a local anthropologist, and its effectiveness insured by poisoning his dinner).

The boarding house where John stayed in Madison is now a private residence. It's a handsome building overlooking Lake Mendota, and the window of his former attic room can be seen on the left side of the roof.

I also walked across the railroad bridge connecting the west bank of the Wisconsin River to Barker Stewart, "Body" Island. This is where Katherine had her experience, and while Eli described it as a pretty spot, that was in the summer. The attractions are less obvious in the tired light of a January afternoon, with scrubby trees poking out of snowdrifts along the banks and the river frozen into blue-green pavement.

The bridge itself is made up of three parts. Two open-work rectangular boxes separated by a middle section with solid metal walls that follow each other across the river on squat pontoon-shaped concrete piers. It's not the kind of local landmark that's likely to appear on a postcard with "Welcome Home to Wausau!" printed across the top, but the scene isn't sinister, just gray and wintry. Maybe the place has a different feeling at night, when thoughts of murdered women and drowned lumberjacks begin asserting themselves.

I stepped from the shelter of the trees onto the bridge's wooden walkway and immediately heard whistling, but this was the wind; there was a breeze coming off the river that caressed your face like the business end of a belt-sander. Wisconsin doesn't let you forget it's winter, and after fighting the temptation to experiment (what would really happen if I touched a girder with my tongue?), I continued across to the island.

There was little there. Just train tracks that disappeared into the snow and stands of tall yellow prairie grass waving in the wind. Nothing that looked like the animated contents of a butcher's case came flopping through the snow, and no dark figures were lurking in the brush, apart from Eli, who accompanied me on my visit.

Katherine, of course, never made it to Body Island. After breaking up with Eli, she had a relationship with John but it did not last. Today Katherine is married and living in another state while John is an interstate truck driver.

Not long after their experience with the Bye-Bye Man, Eli left Wisconsin. He spent several years studying the Romany people in England and Eastern Europe, met the woman who would become his wife in Bulgaria, and today they live in New York City where he works with the mentally ill. While Eli still hasn't had a paranormal experience, he remains interested in strange phenomena and wrote out the account used here. He also showed me the bridge, boarding house, and other sites related to the story.

Visiting these places was interesting but did not provide any new insights. Was the Bye-Bye Man real, in the sense that other people are real? Was he imaginary? Or does he belong to some other category that's difficult to define? Like most researchers, I set out to answer these questions with the confidence of Harry Angel, the doomed detective in *Falling Angel*, who tells his client, Louis Cyphre, that "Nothing's going to stop me from getting to the truth."

It didn't take long, however, before I appreciated Cyphre's reply: "The truth, Mr. Angel, is an elusive quarry."

AFTERWORD: SEARCHING
FOR THE BYE BYE MAN

When I discover lost stories, or new information about familiar ones, it inspires a sense of protectiveness akin to a mother cat's feelings about her kittens. "The Bridge to Body Island," aka "The Bye Bye Man," is an exception. Despite being my most popular story, and a personal favorite, I was just one link in a chain of storytellers. Each one added something and brought it to larger audience, rescuing the story from obscurity.

Of the three people who participated in the séances, two had frightening experiences and were eager, if not anxious, to forget the entire incident. But one of the protagonists, Eli, is a natural-born storyteller. He took the Ouija board experiments, the Spirit of the Board's revelations, and the strange phenomena, and wove them into a coherent narrative, which became the closing event at his annual pre-Halloween Devil's Night party. When it gets late, guests are invited to tell ghost stories, after which Eli sends everyone home with the Bye-Bye Man. I am one of hundreds of people who have heard his recitation over the years; but in addition to finding the story scary, it also made the divining rod in my head vibrate.

A lifetime spent searching for oddities hones one's appreciation for good material. I started early: my mother was an emergency room nurse who worked nights and raised me on hilariously grotesque tales. When she arrived home following her night shift, breakfast consisted of waffles, orange juice, and hearing about the dead woman who sat up straight and was audibly grinding her teeth. Beyond seeing the potential of the Bye-Bye Man, though, my contribution was modest.

I asked Eli to write down a detailed account, I added some context and background, and included it in *The President's Vampire* as an example of the strange-but-true in contemporary life. At the time, I also harbored a secret ambition, which was to see the Bye-Bye Man become part of American folklore.

Publicizing the book meant being interviewed on a series of podcasts and radio shows, culminating with *Coast to Coast AM*. That night, I told host George Noory about the Wisconsin students' adventures with the Bye-Bye Man, Gloomsinger, and so on, and it turned out that the next storyteller was in the audience. And the listener thought "The Bridge to Body Island" would make a good horror movie. And so the process began.

I love horror movies but know that the chances of any movie getting made are remote. With that caution in mind, I signed the contract, obtained the necessary releases, and tried not to think about it anymore; in fact, it was more or less forgotten until the Slender Man appeared.

Call it silly, but I could not watch a fictional supernatural character become one of the most notorious figures in American folklore without a pang of envy and regret. It should have been the Bye-Bye Man out there inspiring children to commit murder; but I sent him to California, where he was being subjected to whatever mysterious alchemy transforms ideas into movies. Fortunately, such thoughts were rare, and I went about my business until a friend called to say that my name was in *Variety*.

After that, events moved quickly. Now, I find myself unnerved by the prospect of attending a movie premiere, and marveling at the story's progress. A monster created, or revealed, through the Ouija board is poised to become the next big cinematic bogeyman, and millions of horror fans will soon be thinking about the Bye-Bye Man. That is *a lot* of psychic beacons.

—Robert Damon Schneck
February 29 (Leap Day), 2016

EPILOGUE

Authors, especially those who write horror and science fiction, are often asked where they get their ideas. A book like this inspires similar questions, like "where do you find these things?" or "how did you come to write about such-and-such a haunting, or this-or-that ghoul?" and even "why do you spend your time on this stuff?" The first is easy to answer because weird stories are everywhere.

Books, magazines, and newspaper columns are devoted to the subject, along with radio programs, television series, countless websites, chat-rooms, and online bulletin boards. These sources collect reports from all over the world and, taken together, create the impression that the unusual is not especially uncommon. Even then, it's reasonable to assume that there's a lot more iceberg down there, with media accounts representing a fraction of the odd, seemingly paranormal, incidents that are actually experienced.

I have no proof, of course. Pollsters rarely ask, and anomalies don't come up in the course of ordinary conversation. Have you ever heard a tired co-worker say that he woke up at 3 AM with a monster sitting on his chest? I do know, however, that when people meet someone like me, with a more than casual interest in strange things, they start telling stories.

- A man sitting at a lunch counter described a light bulb in the attic of his parents' house that answered questions. It hung from the ceiling and flickered a certain number of times for "yes" and for "no."
- While standing on line at the corner grocery, another customer told me about a town in Rumania that was overrun by vampires. He said that the dictator, Nicolae Ceaușescu, sent in troops to restore order.
- A waiter at a coffee shop was hunting with some friends in Texas, when they saw a gigantic hairy bigfoot-type head and shoulders rise up out of the tall weeds and

start towards them. The three of them ran back to
the truck, and almost turned it over getting away.
• While getting my hair cut, the barber mentioned seeing a
hoofed and horned devil in the Egyptian desert. It stood
on a spot where army deserters had been executed.

I've heard more of these than I can remember; interesting, but
unremarkable, accounts of ghosts, psychic phenomena, and flying
saucers, along with numerous urban legends of the "and his sweater
was draped across the hitchhiker's tombstone" variety. There have
also been occasional hard-to-classify oddities, including my personal
favorite, something that sucked the ink out of every ballpoint pen
brought into the witness's house (and may have also been responsible
for tiny puddles of ink that subsequently appeared on the floor).
With the exception of the Bye-Bye Man, however, the stories in this
book came from published sources.

The history of Ransford Rogers, for example, turned up
accidentally while I was looking for a work from 1807 called *Authentic
account of the appearance of a ghost in Queen-Ann's County, Maryland*
(". . . *proved in said County court in the remarkable trial—state o* [sic]
*Maryland, use of James, Fanny, Robert and Thomas Harris, versus Mary
Harris, administratrix of James Harris. From attested notes, taken in
court at the time by one of the council"*), which I still want to read.

I learned about Newark's missing boys from a small newspaper
item that appeared on the anniversary of their disappearance in
1988. I cut it out and saved it for sixteen years before using it. The
clipping spent the time stored in a filing cabinet filled with articles
about lizard-men, squid-things seen living in toxic waste, demonic
possession as a legal defense, and the discovery of the world's first
poisonous bird in New Guinea. Clearly, there's no shortage of
wonders, but how do you decide which ones to write about?

I began by laying out a few basic guidelines. Each incident had
to take place in the United States or what would become the U.S.
(Gloucester's raiders), or under the American flag (James Brown),
with examples ranging from colonial times to today. As a collection of
strange-but-true stories, *The President's Vampire* could include almost

any bizarre incident or episode I chose, but my objective was to find material that was unfamiliar to even the most dedicated readers of quaint and curious volumes of forgotten lore. With that in mind, I collected what was unpublished, distorted, fragmented, incomplete, overshadowed, or buried in obscure books and silverfish-nibbled pamphlets.

This led to long lists of possible subjects most of which could not be used. In one case, my source claimed to have personal knowledge of a traffic accident involving a Navajo man and a skinwalker (shape-shifting sorcerer), but he could not be found. Other stories were discarded because they were thin stuff, like the anecdotes from the barbershop and grocery store, and I wanted something more substantial.

Take "The President's Vampire." I was expecting to write the history of an early American serial killer and living vampire, but after doing the research, it became clear that James Brown's reputation was largely undeserved. He was a murderer and a lunatic and apparently posed a danger to other inmates, but no evidence emerged of either blood-drinking or additional victims. Several versions of the *Eagle*'s vampire article remain in circulation, but while Brown was not responsible for decimating the crew of the *Atlantic*, his real life was gothic enough. There were the years in St. Elizabeths, where discipline was maintained, literally, with an iron rod, the possible connections to Mercy Brown and *Dracula*, plus some uncommon details of nineteenth-century life, like the tattoo-by-tattoo inventory of Brown's body, and a lawyer paid in whale oil. This capacity for illuminating odd corners of the past is one of the most attractive features of the strange-but-true.

The history (or histories) of Pedro, for example, involves economics as well as mummies. Unemployment led to the revival of amateur prospecting and the looting of ancient sites, which probably resulted in Pedro's discovery. These activities were not unique to Wyoming, or 1932, but it was the "cruelest year" of the Great Depression and the appearance of several mummies, and possibly the carved pygmy heads, suggests that poverty made them more common. The recent discovery of another mummy also means that the story is really just beginning. DNA analysis and other techniques will doubtless raise questions that will keep scientists busy for years because once research has started, it never really ends. Which leads us back to a question I posed at the opening of this section; why do I spend my time on these things?

At one time it left me stumped. How could anyone *not* be fascinated by weird things? Years later, I understood that an occasional horror movie or "In Search of . . ." documentary satisfied the general public's appetite for oddities, and that they don't really understand an interest in the strange that goes deeper. Louis Pasteur can mess around with beakers all day and that's fine, what with rabid dogs and everything, but searching for a vintage 1692 phantom musket ball seems to require an explanation. Why, then, are certain people drawn to the bizarre?

Some have had unexplained experiences and/or see the mysterious as a source of knowledge and power. Others consider anomalies to be natural occurrences, little different than electromagnetism or tarantulas, and just as susceptible to study and rational understanding. Then there are people like me who just seem to have a natural affinity for the off-kilter. It may be genetic or the results of Mercury being in retrograde; your guess is as good as mine.

I have seen what looked like paranormal phenomena twice, and taken part in parapsychology experiments, but these were incidental to my interest in the strange-but-true as history. That is what drives the research, and research is the core of my work. Many writers consider it the dullest part of their job but for me it's a combination of Christmas morning, piecing together a dinosaur skeleton, and playing Battleship ("Hey! You sunk my unsubstantiated conclusion!"). There are always new challenges and no way of knowing where an investigation might lead. Presumably, most people write because they have a powerful urge to tell stories, but I do it to tell everyone what I found in those stacks of books and spools of microfilm.

I can't close this without taking the opportunity to thank you for reading . . . and to ask for your help. If you can answer any of the questions that appear in this book, or have any information to add, please write to me. Likewise, if you know of a local oddity, something strange and little known, I would like to hear from you.

E-mail: Damon333@earthlink.net

Perhaps we can solve an old mystery or, more likely, hatch some new ones.

NOTES

Introduction

1. R. DeWitt Miller, *Impossible—Yet It Happened!* (New York: Ace Books, 1947), back cover.

2. Charles Fort, *The Complete Books of Charles Fort* (New York: Dover Publications Inc., 1974), 1033.

3. Ibid., 210.

4. Ibid., 901.

5. R. DeWitt Miller, front cover.

6. "Mystery of the Opera Star: Did Someone Try to Kill Her?" *The Baltimore Sun*, July 24, 1951.

Chapter 1: The Devil's Militia

1. Marilynne K. Roach, *The Salem Witch Trials* (New York: Cooper Square Press, 2002), XLIV.

2. John Greenleaf Whittier, *The Complete Poetical Works of John Greenleaf Whittier* (Boston: Houghton Mifflin, 1894), 53.

3. *Poulson's American Daily Advertiser*, Philadelphia, March 9, 1818.

4. Cotton Mather, *Magnalia Christi Americana* (Hartford: Silas Andrus, 1820), 621.

5. Roach, 195.

6. Mather, 621.

7. "The Cochecho Massacre" <http://www.dover.nh.gov/government/city-operations/library/history/the-cochecho-massacre.html>.

8. Mather, 621.

9. Mary Brooks, "Through Old Gloucester: A Walking Tour Guide."

10. Mather, 622.

11. Ibid.

12. Ibid.

13. Ibid.

14. Ibid.

15. Ibid., 622–623.

16. Ibid., 623.

17. Ibid., 622.

18. Marshall W.S. Swan, "The Bedevilment of Cape Ann (1692)" (Essex Institute Historical Collections, Vol. 117, No. 3, July 1981, 164.

19. John J. Babson, *History of the Town of Gloucester: Cape Ann* (Gloucester: Peter Smith, 1972), 207.

20. James R. Pringle, *Pringle's History of Gloucester* (The City of Gloucester Archives Committee, Ten Pound Island Book Company, 1997), 32.

21. Richard Weisman, *Witchcraft, Magic, and Religion in 17th-Century Massachusetts* (Amherst: The University of Massachusetts Press, 1984), 125.

22. Catherine Finney-MacDougal, *The Babson Genealogy, 1637–1977* (Watertown, MA: Eaton Press, 1978), 11.

23. Roach, 189.

24. Thomas Babson, "Riverdale Story" (1950), 78.

25. Roach, 266–269.

26. Mather, 623.

27. Ibid.

28. Dr. J. Allen Hynek, *The Hynek UFO Report* (New York: Dell, 1977), 214.

29. Michele Carlton, "Kelly Green Men," *Kentucky New Era*, December 30, 2002.

30. John Green, *Sasquatch: The Apes Among Us* (Blaine, Can.: Hancock House, 1981), 92.

31. Ibid., 94.

32. Fred Beck, as told to his son, Ronald A. Beck, "I Fought the Apemen of Mount St. Helens, WA.," (1967) <http://www.bigfootencounters.com/classics/beck.htm>.

33. Ibid.

34. Green, 91.

35. Letter from Mary H. Sibbalds to the author, February 6, 2003.

Chapter 2: Bribing the Dead

1. David Young, *The Wonderful History of the Morristown Ghost* (Brooklyn: Printed and Published by James K. Magie, 1850), 4. Magie may have known the story of Ransford Rogers before publishing the story. He was born in Morris County, New Jersey, in 1827 and lived there till he was fourteen. A short biography of him appears in "Old Settlers of Fulton Co." from the Atlas Map of Fulton County, Illinois, dated 1871 and published by Andreas, Lyter, and Co., Davenport, Iowa. The excerpt is available online at <http://www.rootsweb.com/~ilfulton/1871FultonAtlas/OldSettlers4Text.htm>.

2. James J. Flynn and Charles Huguenin, "The Hoax of the Pedagogues" (Proceedings of the New Jersey Historical Society, October 1958), 241.

3. Young, 3.

4. Flynn and Huguenin, 243.

5. James Truslow Adams, *Provincial Society, 1690–1763* (New York: Macmillan, 1927), 75.

6. Flynn and Huguenin, 246.

7. Richardson Wright, *Grandfather Was Queer* (Philadelphia: Lippincott & Company, 1939), 56.

8. Flynn and Huguenin, 245.

9. E-mail from Ben Robinson to author, March 5, 2003.

10. Giambattista della Porta, *Natural Magick* (New York: Basic Books, 1957).

11. Flynn and Huguenin, 262.

12. Lewis Spence, *The Encyclopedia of the Occult* (London: Bracken Books London, 1994), 18.

13. Michael E. Bell, *Food for the Dead: On the Trail of New England's Vampires* (New York: Carroll & Graf, 2001), 258–260.

14. *The Pennsylvania Gazette*, October 22, 1730.

15. "The New Jersey Law Journal, Vol XVII," (Plainfield: New Jersey Law Journal Publishing Company, 1894), 169–172.

16. Spence, 471.

17. John F. Watson, *Annals of Philadelphia and Pennsylvania in the Olden Time Vol. I* (Philadelphia: Lippincott & Company, 1870), 270–271.

18. Flynn and Huguenin, 247–248.

19. Young, 9–10.

20. Ibid., 12.

21. Donald B. Kiddoo, "Ransford Rogers: The Morristown Ghost of 1788–1789" (Whippany, NJ: published by the author, 1989), 10.

22. Ibid.

23. Young, 8.

24. Flynn and Huguenin, 251.

25. Spence, 125.

26. Young, 17.

27. Ibid.

28. Ibid., 21.

29. Kiddoo, 18–19.

30. Carl Sifakis, *The Encyclopedia of American Crime* (New York: Facts on File, 1982), 311.

31. Young, 22.

32. Flynn and Huguenin, 263.

33. Kiddoo, 22.

34. Young, 24.

35. I. Daniel Rupp, *History of the Counties of Berks and Lebanon* (Spartanburg, SC: The Reprint Company, 1984 [originally published 1844]), 355.

36. Ibid., 356.

37. Kiddoo, 18.

38. Flynn and Huguenin, 247.

39. Ibid., 264.

Chapter 3: The God Machine

1. Slater Brown, *The Heyday of Spiritualism* (New York: Hawthorn Books, 1970), 167.

2. Maurice A. Canney, *An Encyclopedia of Religions* (Detroit: Gale Research Company, 1970), 370.

3. The Foxes were Methodists, a denomination founded by John Wesley, whose family experienced poltergeist phenomena when he was a child.

4. Alan Delgado, *Victorian Entertainment* (New York: American Heritage Press, 1971), 15.

5. Andrew V. Rapoza, "Touched by the 'Invisibles'," from *No Race of Imitators: Lynn and Her People—an Anthology*, edited by Elizabeth Hope Cushing, (Lynn Historical Society, 1992), 69.

6. Emma Hardinge, *Modern American Spiritualism* (self-published, 1870), 220.

7. Brown, 170.

8. <http://genweb.net/~books/ma/lynn1/lynn.shtml>. Bostonians have a saying: "Lynn, Lynn, City of Sin, you never come out the way you went in!"

9. The Hutchinson Family Singers became very popular and their descendants still perform programs of nineteenth-century music.

10. It was probably Mrs. Newton; though Spear's wife, Betsey, and Semantha Mettler have also been mentioned. Nandor Fodor, *Encyclopedia of Psychic Science* (New York: University Books, 1966), 354–355.

11. Brown, 171.

12. <http://www.uua.org/uuhs/duub/articles/thomasstarrking.html>.

13. Brown, 172.

14. Ibid.

15. Brown, 173.

16. Hardinge, 221.

17. Rapoza, 71.

18. Hardinge, 223.

19. Hardinge, 223–227.

Chapter 4: The President's Vampire

1. Charles Fort, *The Complete Books of Charles Fort* (New York: Dover, 1974), 881.

2. "A Human Vampire and a Murderer," *Brooklyn Daily Eagle*, November 4, 1892.

3. "The NIJ [National Institute of Justice] defines serial killing as 'a series of two or more murders, committed as separate events, usually, but not always, by one offender acting alone. The crimes may occur over a period of time ranging from hours to years.'" Michael Newton, *The Encyclopedia of Serial Killers* (New York: Checkmark Books, 2000), 205.

4. Paul S. Sledzik and Nicholas Bellantoni, "Brief Communication: Bioarcheological and Biocultural Evidence for the New England Vampire Folk Belief," *The American Journal of Physical Anthropology*, No. 94 (1994).

5. Joseph Citro, *Passing Strange* (Boston: Houghton Mifflin Company, 1996–97), 220–230.

6. Dr. Richard von Krafft-Ebing, *Psychopathia Sexualis* (New York: G.P. Putnam's Sons, 1965), 157.

7. The Portuguese don't have a tradition of vampires as reanimated corpses feeding on the living. In Portugal they are blood-sucking female witches called *bruxsa* that take the form of birds and attack travelers and their own children. Matthew Bunson, *The Vampire Encyclopedia* (New York: Crown, 1993), 34.

8. President Andrew Johnson's commutation of James Brown's death sentence. T-967, RG59, Roll 3, October 8, 1857–August 13, 1867. National Archive, New York.

9. A "bark" has three masts that are square rigged on the fore and main masts and fore-and-aft rigged on the mizzenmast. This is a slightly different arrangement than a "ship" and requires a smaller crew. "Barks and Brigs, Ships and Schooners." <https://www.whalingmuseum.org/learn/research -topics/overview-of-north-american-whaling/vessels-and-terminology>.

10. Suzanne Hurley, "Shipwreck of the Whaling Bark, *Atlantic*." <http:// www.ocmuseum.org/index.php/site/_article2/shipwreck_of_the_ whalingshipwrecks_bark_atlantic>.

11. *Boston Daily Evening Transcript*, January 23, 1867.

12. Ibid., November 12, 1866.

13. Ohio Penitentiary Prison Register No. 15. February 1889–January 1891, 30–32. It describes James Brown as "Medium built, forehead rounding back and medium; Nose sl. concave, slight depressed, m.

deep; Chin round, Beard black, Boot 9, Hat 7, Hair thin over top of head; large scar 2X2 inches at base of back of head, a cataract on inside of both Eyes, on left forearm in India Ink a shield with three flags on each side, a spread eagle above & a circle band below also R.M.Z. beneath. An anchor on base of thumb & star to left, a heart in center of back of hand, on right forearm a woman with skirt to hip." The "shield with three flags . . . spread eagle" etc., may represent the coat-of-arms of New Grenada. But who was R.M.Z.?

14. *Boston Daily Evening Transcript*, November 12, 1866. Brown's "Nativity" was recorded in the Prison Register as "South Amerika"(sic).

15. "True Bill" found by Grand Jury in case of James Brown, September 11, 1866. With the finding of a True Bill the Grand Jury declares there is enough evidence to hold a trial and Brown was tried as Case #339 *U.S. v. Brown*.

16. Ibid., *Boston Daily Evening Transcript*.

17. Logbook of the "Atlantic." ODHS #797. Kendall Institute, New Bedford Whaling Museum.

18. The Charlestown State Prison also held fourteen-year-old serial killer Jesse Pomeroy, "The Boy Fiend," who spent forty-one years in solitary confinement. Anarchists Sacco and Vanzetti were imprisoned and electrocuted there in 1927.

19. The U.S. Government Insane Asylum is also known as St. Elizabeths. It is still operating.

20. Ibid., Ohio Penitentiary Prison Register, 32.

21. Michael E. Bell, *Food for the Dead: On the Trail of New England's Vampires* (New York: Carroll & Graf, 2001), 18–38.

22. Mercy Brown's story appeared on the front page of the *Providence Journal* on March 19, 1892, eight months before the *Brooklyn Daily Eagle* article about James Brown.

23. Christopher Frayling, ed., *The Vampyre: A Bedside Companion* (New York: Charles Scribner's Sons, 1978), 71.

24. "Shipwreck of the Whaling Bark, *Atlantic*."

Chapter 5: One Little Indian

1. Editors of the *Reader's Digest: Mysteries of the Unexplained*

(Pleasantville, NY, Montreal: The Readers Digest Association, 1992), 39.

2. William R. Corliss, *Ancient Man: A Handbook of Puzzling Artifacts* (Glen Arm, MD: Sourcebook Project, 1978).

3. Karl P. N. Shuker, *The Unexplained* (New York: Barnes & Noble Books, 1997), 151.

4. The Holy Bible (New York: American Bible Society, 1611), 5.

5. Shuker, 151.

6. Various Wyoming newspapers, 1932.

7. Lee Krystek's "UnMuseum: Science Over the Edge" <http://www.unmuseum.org/soearch/over1202.htm>.

8. "Mummifed Dwarf Is Found Near Pathfinder Reservoir," *Casper Tribune-Herald*, October 22, 1932.

9. "Origin of Mummy Remains a Mystery," *Casper Tribune-Herald*, October 22, 1933(?).

10. Ibid.

11. "Mummy Returned to Its Owner Monday," *Casper Tribune-Herald*, October 24, 1932.

12. Eugene Bashor, "Were TWO Pygmy Indian Mummies Found in the Pedro Mountains in 1932?" Date unavailable, may be unpublished.

13. Telephone interview with G.G. Kortes, July 2, 2003.

14. Kate Brown, "Pedro Mountain's Mystery Munchkin" *LATIGO*, Natrona County High School, Spring 1982.

15. Ibid.

16. John Bonar, "The Mystery of the Dwarf Demons," *Argosy*, April 1978.

17. Ibid.

18. E-mail from Jennifer MacLeod to author, July 3, 2003.

19. E-mail from Dr. George Gill to author, August 2003.

20. Bonar, "Mystery."

21. Ibid. E-mail from Dr. George Gill.

22. Harold Kirkemo, "Prospecting for Gold in the United States" <http://pubs.usgs.gov/gip/prospect2/prospectgip.html>.

23. Bashor, " TWO Pygmy Indian Mummies."

24. Bonar, "Mystery."

25. Ibid. E-mail from Jennifer MacLeod.

26. Ibid.

27. "Ivan P. Goodman Dies in Denver," *Casper Tribune-Herald*, November 12, 1950.

28. Bonar, "Mystery."

29. Ibid. "Ivan Goodman Dies in Denver."

30. E-mail from Lee Underbrink to author, July 23, 2003.

31. E-mail from George Hebbert to author, August 20, 2003.

32. "Youth Finds Odd Mummy in Wyoming," *The Sheridan Press*, October 21, 1932.

33. *The Travels of Marco Polo*, translated from the text of L.F. Benedetto by A.C. Ricci (London: G. Routledge & Sons, Ltd., 1931), 283–284.

34. Sunoco, "Three Star Extra" (transcription, March 3, 1950), 2.

35. Ibid., 4.

36. Album 404(?), Field Museum of Natural History.

37. E-mail from Edward Meyer, Archivist, Ripley Entertainment. Inc., to author, August 20, 2003.

38. Brown, "Pedro Mountain's Mystery Munchkin."

39. Normand L. Hoerr and Arthur Osol, eds., *Blakiston's Illustrated Pocket Medical Dictionary* (New York: McGraw-Hill, 1952), 43.

40. National Institute of Neurological Disorders and Stroke <http://www.ninds.nih.gov/disorders/anencephaly.htm>.

41. Anencephalic Babies <https://highschoolbioethics.georgetown.edu/units/unit1_3.html>.

42. Anencephaly <http://www.angelfire.com/mn/michaelashope/anencephalyfact.html>.

43. J. Rodriguez, P. Pérez-Alonso, R. Funes, J. Pérez-Rodriguez, Lethal neonatal Hutchinson-Gilford progeria syndrome <http://www.ncbi.nlm.nih.gov/entrez/query.fcgi?cmd=Retrieve&db=PubMed&dopt=Abstract&list_uids=10215548>.

44. Telephone interview with Barry Strang, June 22, 2003.

45. *Wyoming Epidemiology Bulletin*: Vol. 3, Nos. 1 and 2 (combined), January–June 1997.

46. Bonar, "The Mystery of the Dwarf Demons."

47. Sarah Emilia Olden, *Shoshone Folk Lore: As Discovered from the Rev. John Roberts, a Hidden Hero, on the Wind River Indian Reservation in Wyoming* (Milwaukee: Morehouse Publishing Co., 1923), 6–11.

48. William Allingham, "The Fairies," edited by Arthur Quiller-Couch (1919) in *The Oxford Book of English Verse: 1250–1900* <http://www.bartleby.com/101/769.html>.

49. Maria Leach, ed., *Funk & Wagnalls Standard Dictionary of Folklore, Mythology and Legend vol. 2* (New York: Funk & Wagnalls Co., 1949–[50]), 635.

50. Kevin L. Callahan, M.A., "Shamanism, Dream Symbolism, and Altered States in Minnesota Rock Art." Department of Anthropology, University of Minnesota <http://www.oocities.org/Athens/Oracle/2596/mnra1.html>.

51. E-mail from Dr. George Gill to author, August 21, 2003.

52. Ibid., June 18, 2003.

53. Ibid., June 17, 2003.

54. Ibid. E-mail from Lee Underbrink, September 16, 2003.

55. Bashor, "TWO Pygmy Indian Mummies."

Chapter 6: A Horror in the Heights

1. "Baltimore Steel Industry Called Goal of Reds," *The Evening Sun*, Baltimore, July 11, 1951.

2. Letter from F. P. O'Neill, Reference Librarian, Maryland Historical Society, to author, November 30, 2002.

3. "Fear in the Night: Phantom Prowler Terrorizes O'Donnell Heights Residents," *The Sun*, Baltimore, July 25, 1951.

4. Ibid.

5. "O'Donnell Heights Greets Roof-Climbing Phantom," *The Evening Sun*, Baltimore, July 25, 1951.

6. Ibid., "Fear in the Night."

7. Ibid.

8. Ibid.

9. Ibid.

10. Ibid., "O'Donnell Heights Greets Roof-Climbing Phantom."

11. "'Phantom' Hunters Fined $10 Each," *The Evening Sun*, Baltimore, July 26, 1951.

12. "'Phantom' Looms Atop School; Police Find Ventilation Pipe," *The Sun*, Baltimore, July 27, 1951.

13. Ibid.

14. Ibid.

15. Ibid., "Fear in the Night."

16. Ralph Ellison, *Invisible Man* (New York: Random House, 1980), 332.

17. Robert E. Bartholomew and Erich Goode, "The Mad Gasser of Botetourt County," *Skeptic*, Vol. 7, No. 4, (1999).

18. Telephone interview with Mrs. Adeline Buskirk, December 10, 2002.

19. Jane Bromley Wilson, *The Very Quiet Baltimoreans* (Pennsylvania: White Mane Publishing Company, 1991), 49.

20. David J. Skal, *V Is for Vampire* (New York: Penguin Books, 1996), 62.

21. E-mail from William Michael Mott to author, May 12, 2003.

22. Robert Burton, *The Anatomy of Melancholy* (New York: Vintage Books, 1977), 188–192.

23. Charles Dickens, *The Pickwick Papers* (New York: Signet Classics, 1964), 442.

24. E-mail from Richard D. Hendricks to author, April 15, 2004. For more on Wisconsin weirdness visit the Weird Wisconsin website at <http://www.weird-wi.com>.

25. "The Rooftop Madman of Santa Fe," *Fortean Times* 198 (2005), 4.

Other Sources

Deborah L. Downer, ed., *Classic American Ghost Stories* (Little Rock: August House, 1990), 136–137.

Beth Scott and Michael Norman, *Haunted Heartland* (New York: Barnes & Noble Books, 1985), 326–327.

"Neighborhood Threat" <http://www.citypaper.com/news/story .asp?id=3562>.

"O'Donnell Heights," undated promotional pamphlet.

Chapter 7: The Lost Boys

1. William Morris, ed., *American Heritage Dictionary* (New York: Houghton Mifflin Company, 1969), 1384.

2. Mathur Navdeep, "Revitalization: Newark's Tale of Two Cities," *New Jersey Reporter* (2002).

3. "Milwaukee Is Most Segregated City: U.S. Census Analysis—National Report," *Jet*, December 16, 2002 <http://www.highbeam.com/d06/1G1-95632042.html>.

4. Kelly Heyboar and Kinga Borondy, "20 Years Later, Fate of 5 Teens Still a Mystery," *Star-Ledger*, Newark, August 20, 1998.

5. Ibid.

6. Ibid.

7. Ibid.

8. Tex Novellino, "Newark Cops Get a Promise," *Star-Ledger*, Newark, October 15, 1978.

9. E-mail from P. Antonacci to author, June 19, 2003.

10. Steven T. Walker, "Baffling Case of 5 Missing Teens Still Unsolved," *Star-Ledger*, Newark, September 29, 1991.

11. Ibid.

12. "The Jonestown Massacre" (Brighton, Eng.: Temple Press Limited, 1993), 26. Transcript of the Rev. Jim Jones' last speech.

13. "History of Union Station" <http://www.unionstationdc.com/info/tourismhistory.html>.

14. Lisa Peterson, "Newark Cop's Search for Vanished Teens Temporarily on Hold," *Star-Ledger*, Newark, May 19, 1995

15. Walker, "Baffling Case."

16. Sarah Moran, *Psychics* (Surrey, Eng.: Quadrillion Publishing Ltd., 1999), 10.

17. Ibid., 42.

18. John Hassel and Lisa Peterson, "Cops Digging Again in Case of Five Vanished Teens," *Star-Ledger*, Newark, May 15, 1996.

19. Lisa Peterson, "Psychic Goes Above, Beyond to Aid Cops," *Star-Ledger*, Newark, May 16, 1996.

20. Jo Stein, "Psychic Tours Newark in Mystery of Missing Teens," *Star-Ledger*, Newark, June 13, 1996.

21. Ibid.

22. Walker, "Baffling Case."

23. Heyboar, Borondy, "20 Years Later."

24. Ibid.

25. Ibid.

26. Ibid.

27. Jim Krane, "Charles 'Chuck' Conte, a tenacious detective," *Star-Ledger*, Newark, August 31, 2000.

28. Walker, "Baffling Case."

29. "Longest Missing Person Inquiry—20 Years On" <http://news.bbc.co.uk/1/hi/uk/153230.stm>.

30. Moran, 80.

31. Heyboar, Borondy, "20 Years Later."

32. Ibid.

33. Walker, "Baffling Case."

34. Ibid.

35. Ibid.

36. Ibid.

37. Heyboar, Borondy, "20 Years Later."

38. Mark Benecke Ph.D., "Spontaneous Human Combustion. Thoughts of a Forensic Biologist," *Skeptical Inquirer* 22(2) (1998), 47–51 <wiki2.benecke.com/index.php?title=1998_Skeptical_Inquirer:_Spontaneous_Human_Combustion>.

39. <http://www.blcremationsystems.com/pfurnace2.htm>.

40. Oliver Cyriax, *Crime: An Encyclopedia* (North Pomfret, VT.: Trafalgar Square Publishing, 1993), 101–102.

41. "Five Teens Still Missing 20 Years Later," *The Times of Trenton*, New Jersey, August 24, 1998.

42. <http://www.snopes.com/horrors/gruesome/lostwreck.asp>; Jan Harold Brunvand, *Curses! Broiled Again!* (New York: W. W. Norton & Company Ltd., 1989), 99–100.

43. Krane, "Charles 'Chuck' Conte, a tenacious detective."

Chapter 8: The Bye Bye Man

1. Nandor Fodor, *Encyclopedia of Psychic Science* (New York: University Books, 1966), 232.

2. Ibid., 374.

3. D. Scott Rogo, *The Poltergeist Experience* (New York: Penguin Books, 1979), 57.

4. Collin de Plancy, *Dictionary of Demonology* (New York: Philosophical Library, 1965) 25.

5. *Carrier Dove* (Oakland) July 1886, 171. Reprinted from the *New York Daily Tribune*, New York, March 28, 1886 <http://www.museumoftalkingboards.com>.

6. Ibid.

7. *Oxford English Dictionary, 2nd ed., Vol. 10* (Oxford: Clarendon Press, 1989), 992.

8. <http://www.museumoftalkingboards.com>.

9. Ibid.

10. E.A. Wallis Budge, *Amulets and Talismans* (New Hyde Park, NY: University Books, 1961), 360.

11. Manfred Lurker, *The Gods and Symbols of Ancient Egypt* (London: Thames and Hudson, 1984), 128.

12. Fodor, 48.

13. Ibid., 276.

14. <http://www.museumoftalkingboards.com>.

15. Rosemary Ellen Guiley, *Harper's Encyclopedia of Mystical & Paranormal Experience* (Edison, NJ: Castle Books, 1991), 607.

16. Raymond Bayless, "Ouija Boards: Dangerous Toys?" *Probe—The Unknown,* July 1975, Vol. 3, No. 3, 54.

17. <http://www.demonologyresearch.com/DVDR/Ouija.htm>.

18. <http://www.lifehouse.org/tracts/blbdontgettrapped.htm>.

19. <http://www.evangelicaloutreach.org/ouija.htm>.

20. Mark Opsasnick, "The Haunted Boy of Cottage City: The Cold Hard Facts Behind the Story That Inspired *The Exorcist*," *Strange Magazine,* No. 20, December 1998.

21. "Mrs. Turley Appeals to High Court," *The St. John's Herald*, Arizona, February 15, 1934.

22. Ibid.

23. "Mrs. Turley Will Stand Trial Soon," *The St. John's Herald*, Arizona, February 8, 1934.

24. Harry J. Anslinger, "Marijuana: Assassin of Youth," *The American Magazine*, Vol. 124, No. 1, July 1937.

25. E-mail from Timothy Hodkinson to author, November 13, 2003.

26. E-mail from Helen of Troy to author, November 13, 2003.

27. E-mail from Stephen Jones to author, November 16, 2003.

28. Bill Sasser, "Herbert Singleton," *Raw Vision* #40 <http://www .rawvision.com/articles/herbert-singleton.html>.

29. <http://www.luckymojo.com/bluesmojolenoir.html>.

30. E-mail from Kevin Herridge of the Algiers Historical Society to author, October 23, 2003.

31. E-mail from Louise Punch of the Belle Chasse School to author, January 21, 2004.

32. E-mail from Captain K.L. Shaver to author, December 20, 2003.

33. Michael Newton, *Still at Large* (Port Townsend, WA: Loompanics Unlimited, 1999), 167–168.

34. "$5000 Reward: Who is Cleveland's Dread 'Butcher of Kingsbury Run'?" *Official Detective Stories,* November 1, 1937, Vol. IV, No. 12, 8.

35. James Jessen Badal, *In the Wake of the Butcher* (Kent, OH: Kent State University Press, 2001), 174.

36. "Killers Ride the Rails," *The Spokesman-Review*, July 30, 1997.

37. Maria Leach, ed., *Frank & Wagnalls Standard Dictionary of Folklore and Mythology vol. 2* (New York: Funk & Wagnalls Co. 1950), 881.

38. Martin Ebon, ed., *Exorcism: Fact Not Fiction* (New York: Signet Books, 1974), 244.

39. de Plancy, 139.

40. Heinrich Kramer and James Sprenger (M. Summers edition), *The Malleus Maleficarum* (New York: Dover Publications, 1971), 130.

41. Malachi Martin, *Hostage to the Devil* (New York: Perennial Library, 1987), 436.

42. Donald Attwater, ed., *A Catholic Dictionary* (New York: Macmillan Company, 1958), 390.

43. Martin, 436.

44. Robert E. Gard and L.G. Sorden, *Wisconsin Lore* (Madison: Wisconsin House Ltd., 1962), 13.

45. Robert Burton, *The Anatomy of Melancholy* (New York: Vintage Books, 1977), first partition, 200.

46. Normand L. Hoerr and Arthur Osol, eds., *Blakiston's Illustrated Pocket Medical Dictionary* (New York: McGraw-Hill, 1952), 24.

47. Herman Melville, *Moby Dick* (Mahwah, NJ: Watermill Press, 1985),182.

48. African Americans with Albinism <http://www.albinism.org/publications/african-americans.html>.

49. Newton, 24.

50. David Max Eichhorn, *Cain: Son of the Serpent* (Chappaqua, NY: Rossel Book, 1985), 99.

51. E-mail from Terence Chua to author, November 15, 2003.

52. Martin Bright and Paul Harris, "Thames Torso Boy Was Sacrificed," *Guardian Unlimited The Observer*, London, June 2, 2002 <http://www.guardian.co.uk/crime/article/0,2763,726490,00.html>.

53. William Hjortsberg, *Falling Angel* (New York: Harcourt Brace & Jovanovich, 1978), 155.

54. Roger Ebert, "Angel Heart," *Chicago Sun-Times*, Chicago, March 6, 1987.

55. Dennis William Hauck, *Haunted Places* (New York: Penguin Books, 1996), 195.

56. Robert Anton Wilson, *Everything Is Under Control* (New York: Harper Perennial, 1998), 292.

57. *Philip: The Imaginary Ghost*. George Ritter Films Ltd.(?) Copyright 1974, Toronto Society for Psychical Research.

58. Iris M. Owen with Margaret Sparrow, *Conjuring Up Philip* (New York: Harper & Row, 1976), 15.

59. Ibid., *Philip: The Imaginary Ghost*.

60. Guiley, 444.

61. Owen, 32.

62. Ibid., *Philip: The Imaginary Ghost.*

63. Charles Winick, *Dictionary of Anthropology* (Paterson, NJ: Littlefield, Adams & Company, 1964), 461.

64. Guiley, 616.

65. Alexandra David-Neel, *Magic and Mystery in Tibet* (New York: New York University Books, 1958), 292.

66. Ibid., 314.

67. Ibid., 315.

68. Ibid., 313.

69. Ibid., 315.

70. Ibid.

71. Carroll C. Calkins, ed., *Reader's Digest: Mysteries of the Unexplained* (Pleasantville, NY: The Reader's Digest Association, 1982), 176.

72. Jon Krakauer, *Into Thin Air* (New York: Villard, 1998), 252.

73. Dion Fortune, *Psychic Self-Defense* (York Beach, ME: Samuel Weiser Inc, 1999), 53.

74. Ibid.

75. Matthew Bunson, *The Vampire Encyclopedia* (New York: Crown, 1993), 254.

76. Fortune, 52.

77. James Thurber, *The Thurber Carnival* (New York: Harper & Row, 1931), 83.

78. David-Neel, 313.

79. Mick Holien, "Florence Murders: Officials Release Sketches," *Headwater News of the Rockies*, Montana, November 15, 2001 <http://www.missoulian.com/articles/2001/11/15/export37547.txt>.

APPENDIX I

Entries in the logbook of the bark *Atlantic*.

Wednesday, May 23rd 1866
   Fine weather and breeze from S.E. cruising in different directions. Employed bundling bone. 4 P.M. squally furled light-sail. At sunset short sail. Head by the wind on port-tack. 6:30 P.M. James M. Foster while leaning against a cask by the fore swifter was stabbed and lived about five minutes afterward. John Siars standing near him at the time, said that he saw James Brown (the cook) do the deed. Put Jas. Brown in double-irons, in the forehold. After being put in irons, he (Jas. Brown) said that [crossed out] to Mr. McKennie (3rd officer) in my hearing, that it was him (the cook) who stabbed Foster. Did it with a sheath knife ground sharp with two edges. After stabbing him he threw the knife overboard. At daylight—the I. of Rodriguez—E.N.E.- 30 miles dist. Steered for it. Strong breeze and squally from S. 12 M. Sandy I. E. the reef 1 mile off.

Thursday, May 24th
   Fine weath. and breeze from S. 2 P.M. ship abreast the town. Capt. Wing took a boat and went in. 4 P.M. sent in two boats with the corpse. 7:30 boats came off. Steered W.N.W under short sail. M.P. fine weath. At daylight steered W. with fresh breeze from S.S.E.
   Ends squally.
   Lat. By Obs. 19.40 S.

(New Bedford Whaling Museum ODHS #797)

APPENDIX II

James Brown's letters

James Brown's hospital file contains several appeals to President Grover Cleveland in which he describes the murder as an act of self-defense. He also refutes a newspaper story that claimed the captain had been killed. These may be rough drafts or letters that were never sent and are not dated. The spelling and punctuation are copied from the original.

To your Excellency President Cleveland of the United States of America. I am compeled to appeal to you. On April 1866. I was arrested on the high Seas in the Indian Ocean in the Bark Atlantic from New Bedford State of Massachusetts. We were on a whaling cruise along one of those islands which had been once under the French Empire Roundridge [Rodriquez] I had been the cook of her under Captain Wing from Bedford and he was also one of the owner of the Atlantic. When a whale ship sails from Bedford they always take provisions for three years not exceeding four on these conditions the captain was very close with his provisions and the men generally applied to me for more food. But I could not supply their wants for the captain would not permit me. To your Excellency President Cleveland my reply to James Faster [sic] was that captain [word scratched out] Wing had told me that he had been down into the forecastle and he saw meat bread molasses and other things on the forecastle floor He also told me that he had ordered you to clean the forecastle after we left Trustteen [?] ground on our way to Cruiseset [?] He found provisions wasted by you which could have supported you for two weeks. While we were on the ground of Cruiseset you went to the captain and made another request for moore foods. He have told you that he would see. You know that I cannot do what I wish this Bark is his and I have to obey him what the steward gives me to cook for you you always get that and if you were not so ignorant you could see for yourselves that it is the captains doings and not mine In the first place the Bark is his and he came out to make money and not to lose. He has claims that you wasts his provisions and I should not give you so much for you do no eat it when he gives me commands to make an addition to you food, I will do so with pleasure. You all held me responsible for the captain's deed I have been taught to obey my superior. To your Excellency President Cleveland. James Faster said to me. I will also make you obey me I then said to him it will be a very cold day. [scratched out] Thereunder he struck me with a belaying pin on the back of my head. I fell to the deck when I got up he struck me again. I saw the blood runing on my shirt I said to him what do you mean He then struck me third times I then stabbed him with my knife. I was then put in irons and the next day the captain had the carpenter made a coffin and the deceased was buried on the island of Roudriedge [Rodriguez?] for we were cruising along that island the Bark sailed close to it and the deceased was sent in the boat to the island to be buried When the boat returned Captain Wing made sail for the Mouritious [Mauritius] where the American consul was But he was not there at that time for he was in the United States and I was sent to

Bedford by the vice consul in another Bark belonging to the same owner when I arrived there they took me to the house of correction until the next day I was then taken to Boston to the United States court and from there to the jail. To your Excellency President Cleveland. when I was called on by the judge I requested him to postpone my trial until the Bark Atlantic returned from sea for these three witnesses were my [scratched out] enemies for they were not on deck when this occur. They had been sick all the time while they were on board of the Atlantic they could not work and the vice consul sent them on with me Two of them were Portuguese and they could not speak the English language. The Judge said to me he cannot postpone my trial

Januar 13th 1887

Doctor W. W. Godding
Dear Sir. I humble wish
to recalled your attention
on the subject which I have
demand of you. Dear Sir
I wish to know from you
if you will be so good and
kind has to let me know
what are you going to do
discharge me or send me
back from whence I came.
Your employers run away
with the idea that you gave
me too much privilege and
they had stop what you allow
me. I am a prison bird has

they said. But I am not afraid nor a shame to go back the little english which I now possess I have learn it there and other things which I have learn there. But at present it is no benefit to me while I remain in this condition. Your most humble respectful servant James Brown 3th No Garfield first

Letter from James Brown to Dr. W. W. Godding. (National Archives and Records Administraton)

because it is too much expense to the government and the Judge would not permit my lawyer to put any [scratched out] questions to these witnesses I gave my lawyer nine barrels of oil at that time oil was worth two Dollars and seventy five cents a gallons every one in the court saw that I was shamefully dealt most unjustly they all asked to have my sentence remitted from [scratched out] capital sentence to prison for life all desired this because the witnesses were Portugueses sailors and could not speak English therefore their testimony was not sufficient. Mr. Charles R. Train my lawyer is dead I have been told by Doctor W. W. Godding and also the Judge and the attorney general who had prosecuted me they are in their graves I cannot find them I have received a letter from captain Wing of whom you may inquire resides in Monagausett [possibly Mionagausett] Mass a letter directed to that place will reach him The statement which you have seen in the star June 25th 1885 when marshal Banks brought me from Massachusetts it was a misrepresentation. [Brown refers to this story in other letters] I request of you Your Excellency President Cleveland to give me my release I want to leave the United States

Your most respectfully James Brown 3th

From the United States of Spanish Columbian Confederation New Grennada

A letter written years later suggests that Brown's mental state had deteriorated and may include his original name. Some of the words have been lost in reproduction and others are difficult to make out; the original seems to be written on some kind of wrapping paper.

November 20th 1892 Saint Elizabeth Insane Hospital Washington D.C. I Thomas Azzotte James Brown 5 [?] Henry Thomson James Brown 238 Adam Azzotte James Brown 3 James Brown 2348 He was born in Georgestown Dimmerarada [Demerara, Guyana] But I hailed from New Grannada [Grenada] I will be fifty four years old January coming 1893 I have ___ard Emma F. Cary. Relation and they are also ___ fancy men said that Doctor W. W. Godden send them a letter to Ohio Penitentiary he tell that [?] they must not have Thomas Azzotte

James Brown 5 taken before a boards of Propreates [?] Judge or if they will not send him here. But get men to forge those propreates Judges __ames and make out a false statement and send him here and I will keep him here and you [?] will have all the chances to put him out of the way and they have also said that Doctor W. W. Godden gree with them Eight mounthes before they brought me here and they said that they have [?] his hand Written which he had advised them to [?] do. Just has they had done to have me brought _____ now [?] gentlemen this is the points Do not take [?] him before a board of propreates judges, For if you do, They would not send him here to me Doctor W. W. Godden this statement show that I am not Crazey

(Case files of patients series 66, Record Group #418. Records of St. Elizabeths Hospital.)

APPENDIX III

How dangerous was James Brown?

There is no evidence that James Brown killed anyone except James M. Foster, but letters exchanged between law enforcement, prison, and asylum officials contain several references to him as "a very dangerous man." (Letter from U.S. Marshal's office Massachusetts District to Dr. W. W. Godding, June 23, 1885[?].) The official correspondence does not go into details but Warden E. J. Russell states that Brown was a danger to other inmates and that he did not want to be responsible for him.

Massachusetts State Prison,
Warden's Office,
Charlestown, Mass. Feb. 7, 1887.

Genl. N. P. Banks,
U.S. Marshal,
Dear Sir:
Yours with a letter from Dr. W.W. Godding was received today—Is it not possible that the order returning James Brown can be revoked or that he can be sent to some other prison?

His often expressed hatred of Massachusetts and all of its officers from the Governer [sic] down makes me think that this prison would be more likely to excite him than one where the surroundings are new—

I speak from the information which is at hand as he never was under my charge as Warden—but I cannot help saying that I do not think it safe to put him into the Shops with other men as there is a greater fear of Brown's treachery among the men than the officers of the prison—Mr. Pettigrew the prison Clerk [sic]—and the bearer of this letter,—will tell you of his disposition if you should bring him on, which I shall greatly deplore.

Very respectfully,
E. J. Russell,
Warden.

(Case files of patients series 66, Record Group #418. Records of St. Elizabeths Hospital.)

ACKNOWLEDGMENTS

First, I want to thank my editor, Patrick Huyghe, for his extraordinary patience. Very special thanks to my brother Steve at the Denver Public Library, Lance Corporal Elliott Madison, Chuan Qin, Kathy Keppler, Dr. George Gill, Donald B. Kiddoo, and Richard Hendricks for being so generous with their time, information, and expertise. This book would have been impossible without the help of librarians, archivists, and volunteers working in historical societies across the country, wonderful people who make your search their own. There are also the many writers, scientists, magicians, ranchers, reporters, and friends who contributed in ways too numerous to mention.

These include Michael E. Bell, Bob Rickard, and David Sutton of the *Fortean Times*; K. L. Keppler for the two original illustrations; Dr. T. Peter Park, Loren Coleman, Theo Paijmans, George Wagner, Michael A. Banks, Snopes, Helen of Troy, Timothy Hodkinson, Stephen Jones, and all the members of forteana@yahoo.groups.com, W. M. Mott and fantasticreality@yahoo.groups.com, George Hansen, Walter Hickey of the National Archive at Waltham Massachusetts, the Paramus Public Library, New York Public Library, American Society for Psychical Research, and the American Museum of Natural History. Thanks to Ellen R. Nelson of the Cape Ann Historical Association, Britta Karlberg of the Phillips Library Peabody Essex Museum, Mary H. Sibbalds of The Sandy Bay Historical Society & Museum, Inc., Marilynne K. Roach, Learned T. Bulman of the Morris County Historical Society, Ben Robinson (Illusion Genius), Larry White, Mark Walker (Prof. Horn), James Lewis of the New Jersey Historical Society, Deborah Mercer and Shaaron Warne of the New Jersey State Library, Sally Biel of the Pennsylvania Historical and Museum Commission Library, Sheryl Hollis Snyder of the Adams County Historical Society, Lila Fourhmann-Shaull of the York County Heritage Trust, William R. Creech of the National Archives and Record Administration, Michael P. Dyer of the New

Bedford Whaling Museum, Elizabeth Favers and Charlie Arp of the Ohio Historical Society, Sylvia Weedman of the Bostonian Society, Diane Shephard of the Lynn Museum, Marlynn M. Olson, Nancy Derevjanik of the Enoch Pratt Free Library, F. P. O'Neill at the Maryland Historical Society; Mrs. Adeline Buskirk, Ms. Peggy Antonacci, Barry Carter, Mark DiIonno, and Russell Ben-Ali at the Newark *Star-Ledger*; Ann Nelson of the Wyoming State Archives, Judy West at the Wyoming Historical Society, George Hebbert (who actually held Pedro in his hands), Amanda Bielskas, Lee Underbrink, Jennifer MacLeod and the Greybull Museum, Harvey Wilkins, the Big Horn County Historical Society, G. G. Kortes, Barry Strang of the Wooden Rifle Ranch, Nancy Anderson at the Hanna Basin Museum, Ralph Schaus, Edward Meyer of Ripley Entertainment Inc., Todd Roll, Monica Hill, Erik Solomonson, Museumoftalkingboards .com, Kevin Herridge of the Algiers Historical Society, Captain K. L. Shaver, the Edgar Cayce Foundation, Paul Gambino, Louise Punch at the Belle Chasse State School, and, finally, to the managers and employees of McDonald's. Most of this book was written in a McDonald's at the corner of 86 St. and 24 Ave. in Bensonhurst, Brooklyn.

INDEX

About the Author

Robert Damon Schneck is the author of *The Bye Bye Man*, which served as the basis for the movie from Dimension Films. That book was previously titled *The President's Vampire: Strange-but-True Tales of the United States*. Schneck is also the author of the Edgar Award–nominated *Mrs. Wakeman vs. the Antichrist: And Other Strange-but-True Tales from American History* (Tarcher, 2014). A long-time chronicler of the weird and unexplained, he has written about everything from killer clowns to suicide clubs, and writes for magazines including *Fate* and *Fortean Times*, where he is a frequent contributor. Schneck wrote most of the book that became *The Bye Bye Man* at his regular table at a McDonald's in Bensonhurst, Brooklyn.

More True Stories
of the Strange and Unexplained from
Robert Damon Schneck...

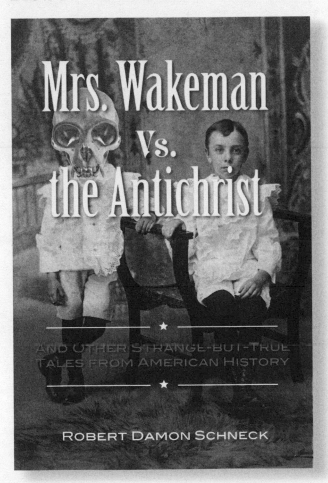